Where Did My Gravitas Go?

A Guide for Introverted Leaders
to Build Lasting Powerful Gravitas
in Any Situation

Where Did My Gravitas Go?

A Guide for Introverted Leaders
to Build Lasting Powerful Gravitas
in Any Situation

Ian Scott

BUSINESS BOOKS

London, UK
Washington, DC, USA

CollectiveInk

First published by Business Books, 2026
Business Books is an imprint of Collective Ink Ltd.,
Unit 11, Shepperton House, 89 Shepperton Road, London, N1 3DF
office@collectiveink.com
www.collectiveink.com
www.collectiveink.com/business-books

For distributor details and how to order please visit the 'Ordering' section on our website.

Text copyright: Ian Scott 2024

ISBN: 978 1 80341 720 2
978 1 80341 985 5 (ebook)
Library of Congress Control Number: 2024948935

All rights reserved. Except for brief quotations in critical articles or reviews, no part of this book may be reproduced in any manner without prior written permission from the publishers.

The rights of Ian Scott as author have been asserted in accordance with the Copyright, Designs and Patents Act 1988.

A CIP catalogue record for this book is available from the British Library.

Design: Lapiz Digital Services

UK: Printed and bound by CPI Group (UK) Ltd, Croydon, CR0 4YY
Printed in North America by CPI GPS partners

We operate a distinctive and ethical publishing philosophy in all areas of our business, from our global network of authors to production and worldwide distribution.

Contents

Introduction: Not Another Book on Gravitas	xiii
Using This Book	xvi
Part One – Thinking	**1**
Chapter One	**3**
Why Bother – Surely You Have It or You Don't?	3
Overview of the Model of Gravitas	12
Courage	13
Confidence	15
Credibility	15
Control	17
Communication	18
Chapter Two	**20**
Understanding Gravitas and Its Siblings	20
Gravitas in Time: A Brief Summary of Where It Came from and What It Means Today	20
More than Authenticity, Charisma, or Presence	23
Authenticity	23
Charisma	28
Presence	30
Embodiment: Our Body Intelligence	32
Chapter Three	**35**
Leading with Gravitas: Adapting to the Environment	35
Part Two – Reflecting	**41**
Chapter Four	**43**
Gravitas: Building a Picture	43
Developing the Architecture	48
An Emerging Framework of Gravitas	51

Chapter Five	**55**
Understanding the Constructs of Gravitas	55
Exploring Each Construct through	
the Temperaments	57
Courage	57
Confidence	60
Credibility	63
Control	64
Communication	65
Chapter Six	**68**
Knowing Your Gravitas	68
Gravitas Assessment: The Myers-Briggs Type	
Indicator®	70
Psychological Underpinnings	73
Chapter Seven	**79**
Gravitas through a Personal Conceptual Encounter	79
Gravitas Assessment: Your Tree of Life	82
Gravitas Assessment: Temperament Scoring	
and Constructs	87
Gravitas Assessment: Goals and Role Models	90
Part Three – Performing	**95**
Chapter Eight	**97**
Meet Your Inner Gravitas Coaching Team –	
Performance Coach, Psychotherapist Coach,	
and Public Relations Coach	97
The Role of Coaching	99
Your Two Selfs	100
Chapter Nine	**110**
The Colors of Gravitas: Situational Awareness and	
Agility	110
The Colors of Gravitas: People	116

    Using Your Gravitas Reflection Diaries
        or Journal for Performing   118

Chapter Ten   121
Using the Somatic Embodiment of Gravitas   121
    Somatic Guidance and Observations   122

Chapter Eleven   133
Situations: Strategies and Tactics Part One – People   133
    Leading Teams and Meetings   135
    Influencing Peers   139
    Influencing the Boss   142
    Social Engagements   144

Chapter Twelve   150
Situations: Strategies and Tactics Part Two –
    Presentations   150
    Anxiety and Panic Attacks   151
    Messages and Storytelling   158

End   163
    Wrapping Up: The Final Piece of the Gravitas
        Jigsaw   163

References   165
About the Author   171

For Erin.

Introduction: Not Another Book on Gravitas

Do you ever feel like others are talking about you with no real grounded evidence? Are you exhausted after being in the company of others, or turn down invitations to attend events if you have the opportunity? Then in part this book is for you. If you have chosen to read this book either in full, in part, or simply to scan, you probably also have a curiosity about the nature of gravitas especially if you are viewing from the afore implied introverted lens. However, some of the people I have met either socially or worked with have often asked, "What is it?" and "Why would that be important?" which are fair questions. The first question in particular is one I have grappled with ever since I was first asked to help develop gravitas with a national body of professional service firm partners. At that time, we had around 600 partners situated around various regional offices with a considerable sense of self-importance and matching incomes. The parking areas were awash with Porsches, M class BMWs, Audi sports cars, Bentleys, and so on, but you get the picture. It resembled the training ground car park of a Premier League football (soccer) club or NFL team. I even recall one partner telling me he had to be careful when visiting clients to make sure his car didn't look too expensive, given that at some point he would need to send them an invoice. However, there was one giant chink in their armor. Ask many of them to talk about anything other than their specialized area such as tax schemes, audit procedures, or telling others what to do, and they often crumbled into nervous finger biting nobodies, suddenly invisible to all those they wanted or needed to impress. At least that was the impression of one of the top partners at the time when he asked me to help. That was in the early 2000s.

Since moving on from professional service firm development, for a while at least, I started to work with engineers, bankers, actors, retailers, scientists, and others, and was not surprised to discover that this disappearance of gravitas at key moments was common to people from all walks of life even if at the time they couldn't find a word for it. In particular, I found that introverted personality types were more vulnerable to losing gravitas. I also noticed that different generations have a varied appreciation of what gravitas means to them. In many cases those under what might be described as middle aged have often never even heard of the term. So, is it relevant today? I believe it is, therefore, let me start with a very brief outline of gravitas as it will be explored in this book.

Gravitas may be a quality with echoes of ancient history but the constructs that are the building blocks of gravitas are assets in everyday life. Sadly, however, many if not all of those constructs abandon us when we need them the most. This book uncovers what defines gravitas for all of us because it is different for everyone and shifts from event and situation constantly, why it goes away when you need it the most, and how to rebuild it in any situation and regain balance. In contrast to a common belief, it is not as simple as you either have it or you don't.

The need for this book is ever more relevant as our work and lifestyles shift dramatically from working away from home to being more remote from others and multitasking our work and home life. Indeed the pressure to encourage many to return to the workplace continues but I sense for many their attitudes have changed as we have become more accustomed to adapting the way we interact with others. The unique feature of this book is learning how gravitas is assembled but also that in order to access our gravitas we must find our equal balancing force of levitas, just as gravity requires an equal and opposing force in physical dynamics. You can't have one without the other.

Introduction: Not Another Book on Gravitas

The nature of gravitas also shifts between how we experience it and how others notice it and feel it from the outside. Tips and tricks to build gravitas are not truly helpful unless we truly feel it. The nature of inner and outer gravitas has to be developed together but the outward perception of others may notice changes before you do. Accessing our true gravitas and levitas is not a quick fix. It takes time and the only way to guide us there is through the little coaching team inside our head. This book teaches a method for self-coaching. It uses the concept of an inner team of archetypal coaches to help us understand others and situations. By developing our gravitas and levitas, we can strive to be the best version of ourselves, especially in challenging moments. Over time those gravitas tactics become embedded and can start to feel more natural. Experience and knowledge can be great assets but they can also act as barriers. Self-awareness, inexperience coupled with imagination can be equally as powerful.

There are a handful of other gravitas books available and many on relatable areas such as executive presence. I have chosen to write in the tone of a teaching memoir because the experience of gravitas is exceptionally personal, and to understand it requires a journey of self-awareness and reflection, and it's the stories from my many students and clients that have helped to develop approaches that have been most useful and practical.

As I write this book I have reached a middle-aged stage in life (my wife suggested that I am much later than this) with the emotional, physical, and professional challenges that were unimagined once by the 40-year-old version of me in the form of anxieties and worries about the future. It only takes a moment, an event, a period in time, or something hard to predict that changes everything, for better or for worse. For me, all of this has happened and there are ideas to be learned, loved, and laughed at to make a gain from disorder.

Using This Book

The book is divided into three parts — thinking, reflecting, and performing. It is entirely possible to read any of these parts in any order or delve into an individual chapter that may be of personal interest to you. However, I would recommend that the tools of reflection to discover your personal gravitas are essential in order to get the most out of any of the other chapters.

The first of the three parts discovers how and why gravitas came to be an important quality for a person because for some it might not be. After all, how can it be that having gravitas is so different to being someone with presence or charisma? Also, one might consider gravitas something with less contemporary relevance than its value in ancient Rome where the word is first uncovered in common use. In order to demonstrate the relevance today the structure of the book tells the stories of my experiences and those people I have encountered through periods of my life which might and may reflect those of any reader from time to time. These represent a contemporary view of gravitas in a time, as this book has been written, when the entire world has recently battled a pandemic that forced millions of people to work from a distance to others. And for those who still needed contact with others required the wearing of face coverings which altered the way some of our senses work when we connect to others. Perhaps for those that are more introverted this might have seemed a benefit but it also allowed them to withdraw more easily, diluting any gravitas effect even further. Through my journey of self-discovery from teenage years through to my later 50s, across four continents, living in six countries, serving in the military, and working across a range of industries, I hope to show how gravitas sometimes appears and where it goes, and how I have tried to understand how the meaning of personal gravitas works for everyone.

Knowing that introverts tend to be deeper thinkers than many extroverts, I wanted to show how a model of contemporary

Introduction: Not Another Book on Gravitas

gravitas is created to help fill in any gaps between a historical analysis of gravitas and the real experiences of it today. I also found during my periods of coaching it in others something equally significant and unexpected, especially for my clients. Gravitas is always positioned as an important quality. But in some situations having gravitas is not as significant as having a balancing quality of levitas or levity, as an equal and regulating force, which in some situations outweighs its sibling. Building a picture of gravitas more holistically will better prepare the reader for the exercises in part two and allow the model to be tailored to suit your strengths.

The second part of the book — reflection — helps the reader discover their gravitas and how it is composed in different forms for every person. The section explores five key areas that sum up our gravitas constructs of courage, confidence, credibility, control, and communication. Each of the constructs is broken down further into additional areas which represent the key behaviors and mental states required of each construct, which are called our personal 'temperaments.' I'll introduce you to the derailers of gravitas. For every benefit there is to building gravitas through each of the key temperaments, it is also possible to have too much of any one area where suddenly one might appear too confident, try too hard, be overbearing and start to become too closed to the ideas of others. We will explore how to build a picture of your personal gravitas using a combination of psychometrics and psychodynamic techniques, and introduce you to an approach called a conceptual encounter to help give meaning to the words you use to describe your experiences.

The third section of the book addresses how to read and flex to common situations we may encounter. It is the section on performing. Firstly, this part introduces the developmental architect that we can all use, 'our inner gravitas coach.' Our coach helps guide us on how to adapt when our performance matters most, when we need our personal psychotherapist and our relational coach that focuses on the relationships we have with others. It is a delicate balance, and where your inner coach can really help you to be the best version of you. It pays specific attention to the role of how our body can influence our mind using a level of somatic awareness and guidance. These key areas are explored: how we lead others and the dreaded world of meetings; how we influence our peers and those we work for, including how we interact with others digitally; how we meet others socially; how we present to others. Ultimately, I would like you to feel able to make gravitas and levitas part of your daily lives.

Part One

Thinking

Chapter One

Why Bother – Surely You Have It or You Don't?

In case you skipped the introduction, I'll recap and expand. One of the very first encounters I had with someone asking about how to develop gravitas was in 2005. At the time I was a director in a well-known accounting–professional services firm. The business was effectively divided into two. On one side was the regulatory audit side, and the other an advisory arm. Ever since the demise of what was Arthur Andersen in 2002 following the discovery of shredded documents relating to the infamous Enron company scandal, accounting firms had to divide their practice between those that provided consulting advice and the one that performed legal audit requirements. They had hundreds of partners in just the one country where I was based, Australia, but the senior managing partner in the advisory arm was not happy with many of them and asked whether I could find a way for them to get this magic ingredient he called gravitas. In fact, he was more direct than that and said, "Give them gravitas!" I recall his exact words as I wrote them down for my own motivation, as he added, "They don't have any, they're awful, they crumble in the presence of CEOs, and only really feel comfortable with the CFO, a person who is much more like them." How to achieve this master stroke of personal change was a mystery to me at the time. This is something most of us can relate to whether we are talking about our working lives, or more socially, having to engage with people we don't know. He wanted them to be more comfortable with anyone so that quite simply they could sell more business and make more money. A fairly crude outline but I knew what he meant by gravitas, or so I thought. In some way I felt I had a near tacit knowledge of what it was. Certainly, it seemed to me that it was something that could be felt, heard, and observed, but I'd never considered precisely and in detail what it meant, and certainly not if it could be developed, especially in an adult learning environment. Nearly 20 years earlier I had heard it referred to as a desirable quality in military leadership whilst serving in the UK Royal Air Force. With a little amateur sleuthing I learned that when my parents had trained as teachers in the early 1960s they were expected to demonstrate gravitas in the classroom. It wasn't taught as such, but apparently assessed, somehow. Therefore, I put together a hasty questionnaire and gathered some ideas from as many different demographic groups that I could quickly access, and together with some more in depth interviews started to piece together a program for the partners. Some of the early basic ideas were backed up following a series of subject specialist partner interviews which revolved around building their wider knowledge so they could engage with others out of their field of specialism, communicate in a more structured and engaging way, and with lots of practice. I partnered with the top business school in Australia and with an acting and business coach who had graduated from NIDA (National Institute of Dramatic Art). Despite the qualities of all of those involved the program was not a success. The primary focus, building and widening knowledge from a business perspective, was on reflection a mistake, some of the faculty we brought in from around the globe were too arrogant and lacked practical experience, and the dramatic art side needed more preparation from me, and more emphasis in general. We had chosen only really to develop storytelling communication skills, which although very important lacked the broader communication skills needed but also any consideration of the mental and physical constructs that make up gravitas. However, despite that my interest piqued in gravitas and whether it could be taught. More research was needed, and I began to draft some ideas about how to investigate gravitas. In practice I found that although the word widely appears in general searches on the

Internet and in academic and practitioner journals, there was very little written about it specifically. It was more of a throwaway term and never really explained. I acknowledge that some of my peers have also looked into gravitas and defined it for their purposes, but I always felt I could explore it from an alternative perspective.

So why is gravitas even considered to be a laudable asset? In 2007, the *Harvard Business Review* published an article entitled "In Search of Gravitas" authored by Gill Corkindale, then the management editor of the *Financial Times*. The article described a situation where an executive sought help to acquire gravitas after having been told they lacked it and that this would potentially derail their career. Gravitas had not been defined or explained by the executive's bosses, and reflected exactly the kind of situation I found as a gravitas coach when asked to step in to help someone. The CEO of the UK arm of a security firm asked me to help him after his boss in the US told him in a performance review that he needed to improve his gravitas. No explanation was provided and no other clues as to what sort of gravitas was missing or needed moving up a notch. I found myself asking the same questions as Corkindale (2007) such as, do we search for gravitas inside ourselves or externally? Is it something observed or experienced, and is it associated equally with men and women? I was not alone. In 1988 Lance Morrow published an essay in *Time* magazine entitled, "The Gravitas Factor" suggesting that gravitas was a mystery or perhaps a secret character. He wrote that perhaps a "a man's character emanated from the densities of the unspoken," adding that it is a phenomenon of power, authenticity, and respect, possibly arising from personal suffering. Dramatic stuff but interesting psychologically. However, while there are many journalists, coaches, teachers, and others with opinions on these questions, there was no hard evidence to support their views.

I personally liked the quote by Leonard Nimoy from the 2016 documentary film about him called, *For the Love of*

Spock, when he referred to a performance by the singer Harry Belafonte who, whilst standing with his hands on his thighs and saying nothing, made the whole place shake with a simple gesture. Nimoy says, "Wow! It was gigantic, what a lesson, if you are minimal that became a big deal." Before reiterating the statement. For me this was also an important lesson when learning about gravitas, especially from an introverted perhaps quieter perspective. Ironically the film's rights were purchased by the film distribution company Gravitas Ventures and I like to think that wasn't a pure coincidence.

In 2008 I moved back from Sydney, Australia, to London. I joined a board consulting firm in central London and set up my coaching business alongside a global corporate education firm. At the same time, I decided that I wanted to study the nature of gravitas and how to possibly coach it at doctoral level. It would allow me to define my own research in detail, and provided a ready sample of clients to pursue an action research approach to ensure my work was as real as possible and enable me to see the effect on live businesses and people performance.

Since my first experiences learning about how to develop gravitas in professional services firm partners, I had created a niche for myself teaching and coaching senior business people, however, because gravitas as a subject and quality was not fully understood at the time I chose to concentrate on the better-known field of building executive presence. As I explain later in the book presence is a related quality but after much more research and coaching practice, eventually, it appeared to be something different and lacked the overall depth needed for lasting impact.

I began my more rigorous investigation into gravitas at a London-based business school undertaking a Doctorate in Business Administration (DBA), and started to flush out a research proposal whilst undertaking classes in statistical analysis and research methods. However, the teaching quality was absolutely appalling — no gravitas there at all! I was used to a standard of teaching and coaching with corporate clients that was so much more professional, and I was stunned that a university institution could tolerate this standard let alone charge me thousands of British pounds. Disillusioned and angry I left after a few months and explained my sadness and disappointment at their performance. My money was not retuned, but I used the few doctoral credits I earned and twelve months later found a perfect doctorate program with a specialized focus of coaching psychology and a faculty used to working with experienced professionals and a fellow group of likeminded middle-aged students. Coaching executive presence gave me an opportunity to begin testing my ideas that gravitas might be a more useful and a deeper subject by asking colleagues, clients, friends, and individuals in other professions whom I met about their experiences and views. Gravitas and presence teaching often seems to be the preserve of dramatic art institutes, schools and academies, and indeed from the angle of acting with gravitas their approach is fabulous. So much so I have attended acting classes to learn how to improve my performance on a teaching stage where my audience observes and participates in the moment. But I also have contracted scores of actors throughout the globe to work alongside me to bring my ideas to life with cultural and gender sensitivity.

My profession meant I led hundreds of experiential learning days with actors, physicians, surgeons, lawyers, judges, sports professionals, teachers, consultants, military officers, and politicians to name just a few. This exposure to experiential learning was the most powerful of all because I believe this was how adults learn best. Not theory, not all talk, but bringing their worlds to life through practice, coaching, reflection, adaptation, and more practice. In fact, this book takes the same approach — recognizing that as readers you are likely to have experiences and opinions, and when we add some deep thinking with research, reflection activities, and practice, real progress can be made. It is not easy but experiential learning provided an ideal way to gather information from others on the following questions:

1. What is gravitas?
2. Is gravitas important?
3. If so, when?
4. Can gravitas be developed?
5. If so, how?

Three very contrasting themes emerged. First, some had never heard of gravitas and almost exclusively that seemed to be age related. The younger those I asked the more likely they had not heard of it. The second theme resulted in answers suggesting that you either have it or you don't. For example, a colleague of mine, Alex (not their real name), said you just have it. However, he also added that you are not necessarily born with it, but you grow up in an environment where you see it more in others, are educated in an environment where it is not taught directly but implicitly considered important, and should be cultivated by those around you. Unsurprisingly he suggested it was more important in established public (private in the USA) schools and prestigious universities. The third theme suggested it was both important and could be developed, and they were also able to be clearer on what it meant to them. Interestingly to me they often represented established professions where they saw gravitas as important in their roles. Returning to Alex, I had observed him in action. He had confidence, a quick mind, an ability to solve problems quickly, communicate in writing exceptionally well, he was tall, and financially successful. I often noticed others were intimidated around him and sometimes I was too. His form of gravitas was rather like a powerful black hole absorbing the energy of everything around it; he seemed to deplete mine and others', which I found interesting. The most significant findings about why he probably didn't have the kind of gravitas I aspired to develop was he appeared overly confident, which felt arrogant, he needed to be right, he preferred imposing himself on everyone, and displayed massive self-importance, much of which could be referred to as narcissistic. The idea that there were different forms of gravitas intrigued me and would form part of my interpretation on what gravitas is and isn't later in my research and subsequently translated in this book.

Perhaps the most infamous encounter with gravitas I experienced was listening to a call, rather than a face-to-face encounter, with the Apollo 13 Flight Director, Gene Kranz. On a Sunday morning in July 2018, my now wife Erin and I were relaxing when the phone rang. Erin answered the call and put it on speakerphone. The call came in from Houston, and then loud and clear on the speakerphone was Gene Kranz. The closest I had ever come to even listening to him was when the actor Ed Harris played him in the blockbuster movie *Apollo 13*. Gene spoke with immense authority and charisma as one would expect but not necessarily in the environment from which he was calling. At the age of nearly 85 he was on the top of his house as the rest of it was underwater during severe flooding in the region. He spoke of this major incident as if it was akin to his washing machine breaking down. He had humor, clarity, wisdom, and so the list went on. He was the personification of gravitas in my mind. You wanted to listen to him, respect, and like him. This was a different gravitas to the one Alex may have had, in my mind at least. However, was there anything that I shouldn't have expected? Gene Kranz was a celebrated Naval fighter pilot, and NASA leader and flight director at probably the most exciting time in space exploration. Of course, he would have gravitas. So, is it about what we expect from someone, their experience and their role? In some ways yes. He had a credibility advantage but with expectation comes a weight.

What if he hadn't lived up to my expectation? There was little chance in my mind that he wouldn't have but I believe strongly that training and experience develops gravitas alongside some natural traits. Knowing your traits is critical to understand your potential but so is recognizing that you have to develop self-awareness and be prepared to practice. Gravitas is not a 'fake it till you make it' quality. And you can have gravitas from a distance, in person, or out of sight. A useful insight to what happened next in 2020.

Part way into writing this book we were some months into the Covid-19 pandemic. This understandably had started to change some of my ideas as many of us were working from home and having to learn how to communicate online with just the top part of our bodies' showing, usually. I had run many courses for students and clients through web-based programs and listened to media training but I hadn't really learned how to set up a camera and convey my own content with any form of gravitas in the way I taught and demonstrated in face-to-face environments. I had learned the hard way during and after an interview with CBS News whilst I was stranded in Mexico earlier in the year. I was being interviewed by a news anchor for broadcast later in the afternoon. The CBS journalist reminded me how to position myself on screen, avoid excessive head movement, waving of arms and hands, and to be conscious of what the background and lighting were like. I had worked with this format before, but under the pressure of a news interview I quickly became an amateur communicator. Filling space with words, not listening, and ending up speaking for 45 minutes in what was a 90 second slot. It's easy to do, and we will cover how to be more effective in this environment later in the book. However, I did watch a master of gravitas on a live call a few months later. Nearly one year into the pandemic I was at home, again, with my wife, and I knew she had a call with colleagues coming up. Previously at the time that Gene Kranz had been on a call with her, she worked with me on occasions running educational events with me as an educator, but now she was involved in the communications and engagement side of Covid-19 vaccine research and medical trials. That morning whilst preparing coffee I heard a familiar voice on a call but this time with a face to go with it, just as the world was becoming more comfortable with distance digital communication. The voice that caught my attention was Dr. Anthony Fauci. Dr. Fauci was the lead specialist to the President Trump administration on immune virus diseases and had become a bit of a celebrity on television, especially when he challenged others' less-informed clumsy speeches and wild notions about Coronavirus. Sure enough there was Dr. Fauci beaming into the lounge, and his pleasing authoritative and knowledgeable voice speaking. Exactly like Gene Kranz three years earlier, his gravitas was as magnetic as you would hope and together with a warm and addictive style of communication. This was an emerging type of gravitas normally associated with people that I had met before such as actors on television or a movie — an on-screen type of gravitas, which more and more of us would need to cultivate. It was clear that if you want to have gravitas you have to demonstrate it both in person as well as through digital communications media.

So why bother? Well, I believe it is quite simply an essential quality, especially for leaders, but also could benefit anyone in certain situations. Introverts have always found the extroverted world exhausting, but the increased need or opportunity to work from home and remotely offers new opportunities for the more introverted. Those more extroverted also have to consider how their impact plays out with others. It doesn't take too much to overdo what could be gravitas qualities in such a way that they become less attractive to others. We might not need to be great within every construct but there are some that really do help us to support self-esteem, manage stress, and to have a positive impact in life. However, turn to Sir Isaac Newton's theory of gravity where an equal and opposite force is needed in the universe, and in my world that meant having levity or levitas. Whilst primarily I have written this book for those in the business world who have to manage and lead others, we all at times need the combined forces of gravitas and levitas.

There are always differing opinions on what gravitas looks like but overall there are more consistencies and agreements on the comprehensive picture of gravitas. Those qualities of gravitas when overly done can create the opposite effect, and it is possible to have too much of any construct that makes up gravitas as a whole. We will also look at different perceptions of gravitas from a gender perspective later because my research found that there were differences which are important when we turn our attention to being adaptable to people and situations. So, now let's look at an overview of the model I developed.

Overview of the Model of Gravitas

Overcoming difficulties leads to courage, self-respect and knowing yourself.

– Alfred Adler

Gravitas has a form of DNA whereby a series of strands intertwine with each other which form the bases for its construction. These bases are defined as the five constructs of gravitas and are formed in the following order:

1. Courage
2. Confidence
3. Credibility
4. Control
5. Communication

The weight of the importance of each is also in the order above whereby courage holds a higher weight than confidence and so on. However, as we will discover later our unique gravitas needs to be tailored to each of us and in turn adapted to any situation we face where we may wish to develop gravitas, but overall, we aim to achieve a balance across all five constructs. When all five constructs are in balance it creates connectivity, which ultimately is gravitas, and it is bespoke.

If you can picture the image of a DNA model you may recall that the bases intertwine with a series of ladder type steps that give the DNA its strength but also an ability to adapt and replicate. With gravitas our constructs are similarly given their strength and their definition but in this case the ladder steps are described as a series of temperaments, which are 'ways of being.' I'll briefly describe each of these to help build a mental picture but also a vocabulary that we can use going forward. As I describe them try to imagine what they mean to you not just as a form of brain function or personality feature but more of a whole body and mind integration of being that is constantly moving and adjusting, and how these may be important to you and whether they are strengths of yours or areas you would like to develop.

Courage

In 1924, Alfred Adler, the founder of 'individual psychology,' wrote that "true strength can never be derived only from talent but from the courageous struggle with difficulties." He emphasized the power and agency of individual action to build inner strength. I similarly found that it was courage that stood out in having gravitas and which is shown as the first of five constructs. Our struggle with difficulties or obstacles may present themselves as people we find difficult or situations that we start to recognize through our history as problematic, and we may have developed unhelpful behaviors and thoughts that need to be addressed. And it is courage first and foremost that is needed to address these, and is the only construct with five temperaments; the others all have four.

The first temperament is to *demonstrate decisiveness without arrogance*. Often the difficulty with courageous decisiveness is that we face having to make decisions without all of the information needed. It is this approach to decision-making where one has to take a personal risk that makes it an act of courage. Experience and training help immensely but tapping into our other construct temperaments can help us be more effective even without experience as they teach us to remain open, read others and situations, and communicate with impact.

The second temperament is to *be assertive with empathy*. Sometimes this is referred to as 'tough love' but really it is about building trust and recognizing that respect is earned. It requires a moral courage and is strongly attached to the third temperament which is to *be authentic and have integrity*. Authenticity is often discussed in conjunction with gravitas, but I hold a caution sign up to those who posit that authenticity is essential. For some as I will describe later on, being authentic is not the best that a person can be if it is not attached to a healthy moral compass and sincerity to match integrity.

The fourth temperament is to be able to *take risks with a positive enthusiasm*. Risk taking is an integral temperament but not a rash one. Sometimes the risk will be a more personal risk for the introvert to speak up and stand out for example. Other times it will be to take an unpopular route as a reflection of one's values and it may not even be noticed by others as a risk, but it will be felt inwardly.

The last of the temperaments is to *find strength to face negativity and failure*. Very few of those reading will not have heard of those key figures in life whose success was not built without experiencing failure, often many times over. The mindset that leads to negativity from failure or criticism from others is hard to overcome but it is so important as a part of courage, and learning how to use negative experiences or attitudes and turn them into positives is a skill that becomes an amazing quality of our personal resilience.

Confidence

Confidence, the second construct, comprises from being *unflustered and composed under pressure*, to *manage and be accepting of uncertainty*, *being comfortable in 'one's own skin' with an identity to match* and to *have purpose and be purposeful*. The difference between having purpose and being purposeful is simply the step from having direction or a reason for being and actually doing something about it. Being purposeful requires action. There is, however, no need to be confident in all situations as that is unrealistic, but understanding why confidence can break down, how to instill it in others, and understanding when and how to employ any of the four temperaments is where our inner coach can help us to navigate how we feel and have that impact on others. In addition, lacking all self-confidence is one of the primary factors preventing us from accessing our personal gravitas, and as such is one of the two most important constructs on which gravitas is built.

Credibility

The third construct is credibility. Sometimes we may hold a credibility advantage. Having a professional status earned through qualifications and experience provides such an advantage. For example, being a medical doctor automatically offers a credibility advantage over some professions where being an expert may be more a matter of opinion. Being a politician for example can be the exact opposite. There isn't an earned qualification that is attached to be a politician, and perhaps a part of this is tied to knowing what motivates someone to do what they want to do. In this instance it is the concept of power. You may have heard of the aphorism 'power tends to corrupt; absolute power corrupts absolutely.' The idea is that the more power people gain the less morality they have. For some the perception is that a politician might be more motivated by power than doing good (I have no doubt some are not like this), and when this perception is held by others it results in having to work that much harder to be shown *to be congruent*, the first temperament. When *one's words and actions are congruent* the shadow it casts builds a case for credibility, a sense of reliability, and ultimately, trust.

Dignity and poise are the second of the four temperaments. When one thinks of dignity and poise you might conjure up an embodied view rather than a mental angle. And I believe this is accurate. The mind and body work together, and when the mind becomes unsettled and frustrated our body reacts and follows suit. However, whereas it can be difficult to change the mind or mood quickly, fortunately it is possible to work with our body to influence the mind. With dignity is also a level of kindness and grace, which are attractive and have levity. The third temperament is to *have imagination and be informed*. Having knowledge certainly builds with experience and education but it is more important to have imagination and to be informed by being open. Openness helps us to be informed and therefore build knowledge but, in some cases, where I have been coaching or teaching with experienced leaders, I have found the opposite occurs. A paradox of age and experience is that the more we have of both the less inclined we can remain open to being informed. When you balance being informed, having imagination, and being open the result is a kind of wisdom.

The last of the four credibility temperaments is *to have humility*. I found this through my research to be one of the most attractive of all the gravitas temperaments, and really it is one of levitas. It balances both of the constructs of confidence and courage, and helps us to be more accessible to others. It has a magnetic field, drawing others to us and lightening us. To have humility requires us to reduce our self-ego and level of self-importance. It requires us to be more empathetic, and works in direct opposition to narcissism. Letting go of our ego is hard to do for some but for others being too humble can make us feel like we have less worthiness and create doubt and feelings of being a fraud and of self-imposterism. Reframing is a critical tool with developing our humility along with letting our inner coach confidently guide us through the development of relationships. In summary the construct of credibility is made up of many temperaments that lean towards the balancing force of gravitas — levitas. There is a composure of assuredness and calmness to credibility.

Control

Control is the fourth construct. This isn't to imply that it represents manipulation or coercion of others, rather it is the construct most closely related to the emotional intelligence aspect of self-regulation. It combines the skills of somatic embodiment with the control of our mind. In order to obtain and maintain the facet of control you need to use either one, some, or all of the four constructs in order to find balance, strength, vision, and poise. To find and recover *balance* is both the temperament of perspective and regaining balance of yourself when you're knocked off course or even knocked down completely.

The second temperament is to *be prepared*, when possible. Preparation can be built through practice or training, and it helps settle the mind and ultimately improve performance. For example an athlete or orchestral musician will spend more time in training and practice than performing. It provides some degree of control over the unpredictability of the events we face. The third temperament is to *build climate*. We have an incredible amount of agency to build climate. Regardless of power. In fact, to build climate, say for example, without role or professional power is 'real power.' You can choose to create a climate of fear or unease, or one of optimism or enthusiasm. If you have ever had to present to a group of people you will be all too aware how much power you have to build climate and how quickly it can erode if you feel ill prepared, or when the mind starts to lead the body into nervousness, anxiety, or even worse, panic. This leads to the last of the four temperaments, to be able change the mood of one's self and *others*. It is the skill of being reassuring, a kind of "grace under pressure" to quote Ernest Hemingway.

Communication

The last of the five constructs is communication. What we say or don't say and how we communicate are often how many interpret our gravitas. The first temperament is to *be direct and precise*. This is not to imply a rude form of directness but to be able to cut through the weeds and focus on important areas. It is worth stressing that I'm not suggesting that being direct and precise is always important. It is important when we are under pressure and need to access gravitas. When we encounter situations and people that put us at a state of unease, being more efficient with our communication can transform our impact. Communication of course isn't just about the words, it is about our style, how we appear and how we listen. The congruence between all of these adds to our authenticity and how genuine others believe we are. In addition, with gravitas our experience and knowledge are important therefore we selectively must decide *when to communicate*, our second temperament, and become efficient editors of what is inside our head. Just as I outlined under the control construct of gravitas, being internally and externally balanced helps us to maintain a *clarity of thought*, the third of the four temperaments. Lastly, the capacity to *adapt and translate* our style and content for different situations and people is what can set us apart from others. We do all tend towards a style and it is often hard to change when under pressure but those with contemporary gravitas do it with ease. Ultimately, we must try to engage and be engaging when we communicate, and increasingly this requires us to do so remotely, on a screen or in written or recorded form. A skill many are being forced to develop as a 'work in practice' but looks like an ever more essential gravitas quality.

The five constructs of gravitas do not need to be equal in proportion and strength. Different situations require different measures, but one factor is essential in all: not to have too much or too little of something. Very quickly too much confidence appears arrogant and less appealing. Too much courage and control can be intimidating and closes our senses down that we need to be engaging with others. And finally, communication that is too direct or lacks precision or misguided experience reduces our authenticity and ability to adapt. It is in this area that our inner coach will ask us questions relating to the quality of levitas, and whether we need to tone down where we are derailing our gravitas. Overall the constructs apply to both extroverts and to introverts, but when it comes to experiencing and developing the temperaments the experience can be very different. Hopefully the practical nature of the book creates visual images of the forces of gravitas and levitas which need to work together to help you find yours. Rather like a seesaw our goal is to find a midpoint where our forces meet. Let's turn our attention to historical and contemporary perspectives to help us understand how and when it is useful.

Chapter Two

Understanding Gravitas and Its Siblings

Gravitas in Time: A Brief Summary of Where It Came from and What It Means Today

Forgive me for indulging in a little linguistic research practice but understanding the roots of a word helps to color in some of the gaps in meaning when we look at gravitas today. When I began studying the subject of gravitas I began with a bias perhaps that gravitas is something desirable for leaders. Be it leaders of people, businesses, or other institutions. At the time there hadn't been any specific empirical studies considering gravitas as either a leadership quality, or as a more generic psychological and physical phenomenon. Academic, professional, and journalistic references share one thing in common: gravitas being mostly a desirable quality. They also suggested that if leaders lack gravitas, it may damage their career in some way and/or the impact they have on others. I also learned that not everyone thought it was necessarily desirable. Some thought it was a dated term not suitable for the modern world. I didn't agree. It's relevant but it has evolved.

The Oxford English Dictionary simply defines gravitas as:

Dignity, seriousness or solemnity of manner.

Where other descriptions, rather than definitions per se, have been proposed, which is not frequently, they tend to offer a different slant with most alternatives agreeing that the Latin root of the word gravitas appears to be something important, relating to weight and heaviness and later to a gravitational force. Continuing on with our etymological enquiry.

The word 'gravitas' first appeared in ancient Latin texts during the time of the Roman Empire. It was prominent between the first and third century AD and is often described as meaning a quiet dignity, seriousness, and duty (Aguilera-Barchet, 2015; Ware, 2014), very similar indeed to the Oxford definition above. It was cited as one of the virtues of man (we'll address that gender slant later) that signaled status in society, and was a mix of inner character and outer conduct that emerged through life as a result of observing others and receiving guidance. That complexity of an inner and outward character that emerges through life, rather than something bestowed upon a born trait, becomes important because I will suggest that it can be learned. Indeed, the Roman Emperor Marcus Aurelius stated that, "gravitas was within one's own power through the development of dignity, sincerity, temperance and carrying yourself with authority" (Kamtekar, 2010). Grant (1996) and Pedersen (1993), describing the foundation of modern physics, also use the word gravitas rather than gravity, stating that there: is an "inner gravitas or heaviness" that connects the planet. When in 1687 Sir Isaac Newton introduced the term gravity, it was probably borrowed from this sense of force, which perhaps is why contemporary perspectives of gravitas continue to believe a sense of 'weight' is also important. However, his third (of three) law of gravity includes some fascinating potential clues to help frame personal gravitas. He stated that when "two objects interact, they apply forces to each other that of equal magnitude and the opposite direction." This is why planets don't simply spin off into different parts of the universe or another galaxy. The equal and opposite force is a lightness to balance weight. One without the other equals no balance. Some of the ancient Roman terms to describe gravitas as a virtue may not be used literally so much today, but the association to values, ethics, character, and morality has received significant academic interest, especially in the fields of authentic and charismatic leadership reviewed later. As Brett and Kate McKay (2017) state on authentic gravitas, "In ancient Rome, four virtues were considered the chief pillars of excellent manhood and worthy leadership — none of which have a single word in English that entirely encapsulates their full meaning: pietas (duty, religiosity, loyalty), dignitas (dignity, status, influence, prestige), virtus (valor, manliness, excellence, courage, character), and gravitas (weight, seriousness, dignity, importance). Of these four celebrated virtues, the last is the one that has found its way into our modern language in its ancient, unaltered form." Today, the Oxford English Dictionary definition is accompanied with an explanation that it is derived from the Latin, 'gravis,' meaning serious. It appears from the above ancient translations that gravitas is the alignment of one's inner thoughts and outer expression in a social context that values seriousness, dignity, and a duty to others or society.

Ancient texts described earlier noted gravitas as a virtue in males but both Fairhurst (2005) and Broussine and Fox (2002) have suggested that gender is a differentiating factor. They observed that women sometimes lack gravitas especially when they "defer to their male colleagues." The Broussine and Fox (2002) study of leader attributes in politics felt that women were told more often than male counterparts that they lack gravitas and charisma following interviews for leadership positions. It posed an interesting thought that there may be a gender connotation with gravitas, and I was always keen to understand both genders' perspectives on any relevance of gravitas to them and if there were any differences in how they defined and saw it, and the benefits and risks with gravitas.

From a more contemporary perspective, the concept of gravitas has been recognized as an important leadership attribute (Duignan, 2002; Eagly, 2005; Gardiner, 2011; Apuzzo, 2006; Dagley and Gaskin, 2014; Kets de Vries, 2015). However, in all of these articles there were never any specific studies undertaken to define the term in any real detail or how it is developed. Duignan (2002), Eagly (2005), and Gardiner (2011) wrote that gravitas is an important quality, but they only connected it to the idea of authentic leadership, which was the focus of their interests.

Consequently, this book I felt must try to address these gaps historically and tackle different gender perspectives. As I have emphasized, during my experience working specifically with introverts building gravitas skills, they not only like to understand the historical connections that gravitas has with human behavior but also how it compares and differs with other related qualities that are now found as the subject of other teaching based books and therefore I would like to layout those contrasts for the reader in the next section.

More than Authenticity, Charisma, or Presence
Authenticity

The only person with whom you have to compare yourself is you in past.

– Sigmund Freud

The Oxford English Dictionary defines authenticity as:

the quality of being genuine or true

Authenticity is often linked to the phenomenon of gravitas (Duignan, 2002; Apuzzo, 2006; Gardiner, 2011). In contrast with gravitas, however, the concept of authenticity has been widely researched (Avolio and Gardner, 2005; Avolio et al., 2004). It has captured the imagination and been a part of or at the center of many interesting business leadership and self-help books. I have been interested in the link between authenticity in relation to leadership and virtues as associations with gravitas since the beginning of my coaching work. For over ten years I ran an exercise which we will cover in more detail later on that seeks to understand where we get our behavior, motivations, and values from. It is an approach to psychology called psychodynamics, and as grand as the title is, it really is a simple exercise in systematic self-awareness, which pays particular attention to our subconscious throughout life to gain an understanding of our conscious behaviors. However, it is surprising how unaware many of us are of our true selves, but also how much we often fear the true version of us. In addition, our professions often require a type of behavior or trait. Consider a typical job advertisement and the requirements they seek as desirable for an employee. Words such as trustworthy, dedicated, team player, empathetic, quick learner, dependable, resilient, and flexible are all personal traits and attributes I have seen not only as desirable but as requirements. And yet, as quick as many of us are to agree, "Oh yes I have those in abundance," the authentic reality is that many do not. Many of my clients, especially those more introverted, are not ideal team players and find empathy difficult. I have worked with lawyers and bankers whose primary goal is to earn more than their peers, and journalists who aim to out compete those around them, hoping for the best publicity. Their authentic self might actually not be that nice! I've run experiential learning exercises based on the process of learning for medical doctors. It's a fascinating process but many of the authentic versions of the doctors I worked with did not have the qualities that Apuzzo (2006) suggested: that surgeons leading a medical team should have the integrated qualities of gravitas, severitas, veritas, and virtus. These terms translated mean: seriousness, morally guided, sincere, and truthful. For example, I have a severe eye disease which is incredibly distressing, but one of my ophthalmology doctors had zero empathy, rarely asked me questions; often I had no idea if an appointment had ended or not even after he had vanished for 15 minutes or so leaving me sitting in the dark, and I was left completely unclear about his level of truthfulness regarding any diagnosis and prognosis. All I can do is guess that I am fighting blindness, with no idea of the time that I have left, what I am supposed to do from a health perspective, and if the permanent optic nerve damage in one eye will eventually affect the other eye. Certainly, I can literally see that my vision changes daily, which poses quite a challenge when it comes to writing a book! He had a certain weight of gravitas from an earned credibility perspective but many of the other temperaments of gravitas, I found, he was missing. His authentic self did not instill confidence in me — I questioned his morality, his truthfulness, and in some ways his sincerity which as I shall explain appears important for authenticity but even more so to have gravitas.

Authenticity is considerably more complex than being true to oneself. Rather like my understanding of gravitas it is both multidimensional and complex. One of these most interesting dimensions is that of being sincere (Trilling, 1972). Sincerity is both an inner and outer quality, and being sincere aligns with my temperament of congruence where there needs to be an alignment between how we use words, values, emotions, and beliefs, and our inner thoughts. One complication we will discover is that how others perceive our authenticity is not as simple as it might seem. We have all had colleagues, acquaintances, friends, and family members that we think just don't understand us. They don't get us, and god forbid, don't even like us! Authenticity alone is not enough because of the judgement of others.

Baron and Parent (2014) provided a useful dichotomy, which was helpful in understanding gravitas by separating the philosophical and psychological explanations of authenticity. They put forward that the alignment between self, outward expression, and how others receive and interpret authenticity is a philosophical stance. You need to understand others to help appreciate how and why others may each see you differently, and how that may differ to how we see ourselves within the context of time and situation. They defined authenticity through a combination of individual virtues and ethical choices that manifests as integrity. Lindholm (2008) agreed that authenticity is connected to the demand of honesty and integrity from others. This appears to suggest that it is the interaction with others that is most significant, and supports the idea that leadership and followership are equally important, such as Goffee and Jones' 2008 book, *Why Should Anyone Be Led by You?* The last two points are important. The role of followers as interpreters of one's expression of honesty, sincerity, and integrity are perhaps the most important factor when it comes down to outward gravitas. Secondly, being true to one's self and ensuring outward expression is aligned to our inner thoughts and beliefs. Those two concepts of follower interpretation and alignment of our thoughts and feelings with our expressed self are useful to help us understand the experience of contemporary gravitas.

The recent interest in positive psychology (Seligman and Csikszentmihalyi, 2000) has helped to increase the interest in authentic gravitas, especially within the realm of leadership. Simon Western (2012) described the increased interest in something he calls the "celebrated self," inspired through the work of Rogers (1951) and Maslow's well-known hierarchy of needs (1943). This renewed interest in being all that we can be has created more self-reflection but also insecurity. After all, once we discover our limitations when we have been told to maximize our potential, what happens when we can't do it? It results in personal emotional damage. By the way, if you want to test your personal attitude towards positivity try an exercise from Susan Jeffers' book, *Feel the Fear and Do It Anyway*. What you need to commit to is to try not criticizing or complaining about anything for week. I've tried it a few times and wow it is difficult! Incidentally, introverts often have a knack for self-criticism, and under pressure have a tendency to project this onto others, which can make this exercise even harder.

So, when we think of authenticity and authentic gravitas we have to be careful. If one is "never entirely authentic or inauthentic" (Erickson, 1995), the thinking should be more towards "achieving levels of authenticity." As a result, I would encourage the reader to orientate their thinking around so that it is not a question of having or not having gravitas, but rather, levels of gravitas. In which temperaments of gravitas am I strong, and where am I weaker?

When facing challenging and turbulent times, tough decisions require greater integrity in decision-making and to be honest with others when the pressure is high. To do this, leaders will need a high degree of self-awareness, empathy, and courage to express themselves. Guignon (2004) emphasizes that both courage and integrity are needed to lead, and to do so requires a degree of leadership autonomy and personal dignity. As I discovered, gravitas is a quality of dignity, and being sincere.

There are some other complications related to finding gravitas through your authenticity in a leadership position. Where you work, what you do, and the culture you are around are not always things you can change. They often constrain us. Having integrity is one thing but if where you work does not allow you to say and act on what you think you face a challenge in being authentic which is why gravitas matters more. As Hannah Arendt's concept of uniqueness (1993) is described she warns that the knowledge of the self as a basis for authentic awareness and development is flawed and is often a "case of mistaken identity," providing a poor indication of "a person's ability to enact authentic leadership."

Charisma

I want to address the idea that charisma could or should be a part of gravitas. Most of us would like the idea of being labelled charismatic but is that a sensible goal or even achievable? As I explained earlier in the section, trying to be the "celebrated self" might be a very negative psychological experience.

I have made the statement in this book that gravitas is a requirement of leadership. Relying on authority alone is insufficient. For example, a good friend of mine who served as an officer in the British Army suggested that one of the biggest leadership challenges as a young officer is building relationships and earning respect. Positional power alone is not enough. In fact, it sometimes makes it harder. He said to think of it as building a personal bank account balance with those around you. The more you invest the better your chance of leading effectively. The more you use positional 'rank' to lead, the quicker you deplete your account. In fact, every time you used your position of power, you would use almost three times the amount of the same currency you invested in building relationships. Using gravitas is the key to invest in that bank account, and it is more than simply being authentic and having charisma.

Some have put forward that there is a link between the concept of gravitas and a leader's charisma (Broussine and Fox, 2002). However, in general I feel there is a stronger relationship with charisma and power. Brian Klaas for the UK *Sunday Times* wrote in an article entitled, "Why we always get the wrong political leaders — how to get the right ones," that those attracted to power tend to be the most corruptible, but I also think they are equally attracted to the idea that they are charismatic. I am sure anyone reading can imagine the type of people who would fall under the label as having the 'dark side of charisma.' However, it is the only other leadership area together with authenticity that stresses the importance of followership, the outward interpretation of others of how important the social environment is. The reason I include that is because when we practice how to develop our gravitas we will need to be able to read social environments, as this gives us context, and to read how others read us.

So, for some people who interpret our gravitas, charisma may not be important at all and may indeed deplete some of our gravitas as I shall try to explain. Understanding the position of the so-called 'follower' has helped me to form a model of contemporary gravitas because the follower cannot be ignored. Is there a danger with gravitas that there is also a dark side to gravitas? There was a wonderful television series with the same title some years ago and one entitled *The Dark Charisma of Adolf Hitler*, and a TED talk and a similar *Harvard Business Review* article. You get the point. If charisma can be dangerous because it can build immense authority and influence followers, perhaps gravitas can do the same as well. In fact the television documentary I refer to showed that Adolf Hitler practiced his theatrical physical movements again and again, especially the use of his arms and hands to build his type of charisma, but if you recall my note earlier referencing the actor Leonard Nimoy, he had a realization that it was being minimal that was a big deal. So we have to be careful with building our gravitas especially if we are animated and expressive, which introverts can also be, to ensure that we also connect to a moral compass and have a positive focus on others.

Fanelli and Misangyi (2006) identified traits, values, and beliefs and behaviors that were "desirable and legitimate to develop" and hypothesized that once understood could lead to higher levels of self-confidence and motivation in followers and admiration for their leaders. For example, how do you measure the effect of someone's gravitas? As a comparison, when charisma was used as measurement tool in leaders it was found that when an organization performed well, followers perceived their leaders as charismatic (Agle, 2006). Where an organization did not perform well, followers did not attribute charisma to their CEO. The fickle nature of others' perceptions is one of the most difficult to manage when you try to develop gravitas. Just when you think you have mastered it a situation will come along and humble you. That is where the construct of courage and temperament of strength to face negativity will matter. The best way to address this is to base gravitas on the principle that it is a quality that is unique to each individual, just as studies on charisma have concluded.

Presence

The last topic that I want to introduce is the one that I actually first started teaching widely in business and I believe is most closely related to gravitas. Presence. Some of those who work in my field believe that presence is one of the key components of gravitas and I can understand why. After all, presence appears initially to share a similar set of characteristics as gravitas. It is a term widely used by practitioners and journalists, and there is dearth of coaching businesses and self-help books dedicated to executive presence. It must have quite an appeal. To be present is actually one of the hardest things to do when you coach someone, especially and ironically when you are coaching that topic. You need to be 'in the moment' with the client simultaneously reflecting on the process, what might happen next, and forming questions. Others make the link between presence and mindfulness, but in my opinion, there is only one standout area of work on presence and that is taught and written by Patsy Rodenburg. The reason I particularly cite her work is its connection to positive energy and how to use it for success, and it is an area of work that inspired me, especially when gravitas is connected to gravity, possibly the most powerful energy force surrounding us. She has primarily been a teacher, coach, and mentor to actors, many of whom are familiar to all of us, and it is no surprise that I also have been inspired by the actors I have worked with to help bring my ideas to life.

The link between presence as an energy and gravitas as an energy also makes sense to me when I refer to forces of gravity having an equal and opposing force, levity. To have gravitas is to be able to draw and attract others. However, presence is different to me. To have presence is to be noticed in a positive way. It does have an impact on others and moves around just as our gravitas field does. It also includes the connection between the mind and body. But it does not necessarily include the gravitas of knowledge, purpose, humility, imagination, and experience, which in the case of knowledge as Marcus Aurelias spoke of is something that is earned and learned often through the wisdom and guidance of others. I also would maintain that one can access presence much more easily and thankfully perhaps than gravitas. The reason why presence may be more accessible is the requirement to develop an inner belief and worthiness of gravitas qualities as well as the outward expression that matches it. Presence can be demonstrated and felt but rather like a muscle it will return to its non-presence state unless it is fully developed from within. Presence has a muscle memory but with time and training it can change and evolve into what I see as the wider set of gravitas qualities. The idea of faking until you make it can be a useful way of coping in the moment, but it won't result in lasting personal change quickly.

What have we learned? Authenticity is important but not completely; charisma can be very powerful, but it has a dark side; and it seems nearly impossible to coach yourself to be more charismatic, inwardly at least. If you have charisma, it is a tremendous gift but needs to be used with care. And finally, presence is wonderful. It's accessible to everyone and has some characteristics it shares with gravitas, but it lacks depth and others will be able to detect that. Especially those you wish to have greater impact on; rather unglamorously I refer to them as followers, but really, they are anyone you have in your mind. And so, as I wrap this section up, I want to signpost a significant way forward before we reflect on our gravitas: the importance of something called embodiment.

Embodiment: Our Body Intelligence

Throughout this book I have said that the mind and the body cannot really be separated. Any sort of work on the development of thoughts, feelings and behavior must also be grounded in bodily interaction (Landau et al., 2010; Ladkin and Taylor, 2010; and Meier et al., 2012). Embodied approaches to coaching simply add more depth and ultimately more of a lasting impact. It is also much more fun to coach gravitas ourselves as we shall see.

This is more than body language despite it being an interesting topic alone. I have also stressed that the environment where we wish to build gravitas is essential to take into account. That reaction to the interaction with the environment where leaders are expected to lead others is all bound up within the body (Dinh, Lord, and Hoffman, 2014). What this can mean is that the physiology and morphology of the body is really the first noticeable conscious reaction we have to environmental pressures. For example, I recall whilst living in North London that there was a problem with what were and probably still are known as 'moped gangs.' I'd watch unsuspecting tourists and day trippers emerge from the Highbury and Islington tube station and walk towards Holloway Road and the area around Arsenal Football Club's Emirates Stadium, and have their expensive mobile phones yanked from their hands mid-call by the rear passenger on a moped, oblivious and shocked rigid by the attack. I've watched people in stores similarly attacked and mopeds rammed into windows, and knife and machete attacks. Sounds nice doesn't it! Well often I used to take a shortcut from my home in Upper Street through the local housing 'estate' to get to my printers. The estate is where the gangs tended to linger, and avoiding it took at least 15 minutes longer. So, I always took the shorter route, walking quickly and carrying very little. The thing was every time I turned a corner and saw creepy gang members loitering, I instantly felt my body tense, my breathing rate increase, a need to walk faster or even run, turn back or do whatever necessary to not be involved or attract attention. Losing all my presence perhaps and intentionally so. The point is I noticed the physiology first before the mind started weighing up risks and actions. It is what many of the readers will have heard of, the 'fight or flight reaction.' A survival instinct governed by the amygdala.

The amygdala is about the shape of an almond and there are actually two of them in the medial temporal lobes of the brain. They are involved in sensing, perceiving, and regulating emotions. Although this covers all emotions, the most interesting is the reaction to fear and anxiety. And it doesn't have to represent life and death situations. How many of you reading this have ever tried to disappear? This could be in a classroom, a presentation, at a comedy club, or simply to be alone. Your body reacts instantly, and depending on whether the disappearing act is a response to anxiety or fear the amygdala kicks into action and so do the prefrontal cortex and anterior cingulate cortex. The result is we find it difficult to focus, except from how to escape, our ability to evaluate shuts down, and our memory gets disrupted. Especially short-term memory. Over time extended anxiety to certain triggers can actually alter the neurological pathways in our brain. Effectively reconfiguring it. Like a form of brain rewire.

Consider a typical business situation where leaders may often encounter what is known as an 'amygdala hijack' — the presentation. It could be a presentation to just a few people or to a huge auditorium. Many, many people are terrified of them. I'm a qualified teacher, and have taught and presented to large groups for more than 30 years, and still I sometimes encounter a sudden amygdala hijack. Almost without warning it happens. And yet the warning signs are already there, especially physiological sensations triggered by the mind. Breathing rate, body temperature, tense muscles and then fear. Concentration goes and the words that come out your mouth don't seem to feel real or heard by yourself. It seems impossible to think clearly and read the reactions of others. It can build from anxiety and fear into a full-blown panic attack, the need to physically escape. I know, I've suffered from panic attacks for as long as I can remember, and how on earth I ended up doing what I do as a profession seems ridiculous sometimes. But in fact, it has saved me from lifelong attacks, and I will share with you later in the section on "Performing" the approach to manage this, rewire your brain, and release the essential oxytocin brain chemical needed to counteract it.

Fortunately, our embodied architecture offers an alternative insight into how to use self-stabilizing physical techniques rather than cognitive conscious processing where self-regulation is needed (Landau et al., 2010). In turn, this may have an effect on how you perceive and lead others and adapt to the environment. As a result when you are presenting rather than conversing your only means of reading the space you are in is to read the physiology of others. So, you need to be both a mind and body reader. The problem with doing both is that the body takes in far more information than can be consciously perceived (Norretranders, 1998). Every second a human mind and body takes in 11 million pieces of information, but only 40 pieces of information are perceived consciously. The body and mind filter information selectively (Wilson, 2002), but much of the unconscious information is observable in our bodies. The responses in the body are known as somatic markers (Damasio, 1994). The embodied somatic markers provide guideposts to our emotional regulation (Ratener, 2014), and we will learn how to use the body to regulate the mind, for both gravitas and its opposite force, levitas, later in the book.

Chapter Three

Leading with Gravitas: Adapting to the Environment

Out of your vulnerabilities will come your strength.

– Sigmund Freud

In the previous section I wrote about the importance of the environment and our body's reactions; the somatic markers that tell us about the state of mind; and prior to that, how we cannot separate a quality such as authenticity or gravitas from the environment where we live and work. The environment in which my clients, business leaders, operate in constantly changes, and at a faster rate than ever before at a macro level and with a knock-on effect at a micro level. For example, whilst I was writing my early drafts of this book the Covid-19 pandemic was tightening its grip with lockdowns in most places globally with many having to learn to work from home for the first time. We had to learn to relate to others differently, communicate, motivate, and organize ourselves differently. Even in our post pandemic world huge numbers of office places lay empty, and for some the working from home environment was sustained, for others it became a hybrid model; many people left the work force, and many businesses did not survive. We have had to adapt.

The argument for this form of accelerated and unimaginable change is encapsulated in an acronym, VUCA, which was increasingly being used in my ecosystem as an educator since the early 2000s. The US military created the acronym to describe a disorderly world which stood for volatility, uncertainty, complexity, and ambiguity. Perhaps that is the environment in which we have always lived, but it is argued that the speed and depth of each of the four dimensions is increasing. As a result, we need to develop tactics and practice to adapt and lead others. The many qualities of gravitas explained in this book offer strength to interact with others in the VUCA world. I have taught many workshops on leading in a VUCA world because the situations in which both presence and gravitas are tested under pressure occur when we encounter volatility, uncertainty, complexity and ambiguity. In 2007 Nassim Taleb wrote a book that the UK's *Sunday Times* described as one the twelve most important books since the Second World War: *The Black Swan*. The book raises the point that we should always expect the unexpected, the unimaginable. In it he describes a way of being called "anti-fragile." A state that we can gain from disorder. The Covid-19 pandemic was a black swan, and learning to become anti-fragile took center stage. Since then we have also had Russia's invasion of the Ukraine, and even now as I write Vladimir Putin has employed an academic to advise him on future actions who has written that a single nuclear strike on somewhere in the EU may be necessary to arrest any thoughts of action from the USA. An unimaginable action but another possible black swan event.

 Refocusing on ourselves, any effort to build gravitas requires us to know our own fragility or fragilities. At first glance the idea of being fragile might be seen as having weaknesses. However, we all have weaknesses and knowing ourselves deeply is part of the process of building the temperaments of gravitas we will need sometimes. Where to adjust our stance, our viewpoint, and our mental models is part of the flexibility of having gravitas. Those that see themselves as having gravitas often don't see themselves as weak in any way. They almost regard themselves as flawless, like most narcissists do. They do not ever believe they may be at fault, because, it's your fault, always. When we discuss the importance of role models and mentors later, one task will be to ensure you don't mistakenly put your faith in a narcissist! Those that know us really well, a partner, a parent or a long-term friend, are often the first to notice our flaws. They usually have little fear telling us what they think of us, and it is based often on years of familiarity, and they are a first-call when building a picture of your strengths and fragilities. Embracing our fragility is essential, and disorder is a part of living a human life. We may try to create order to manage and build anti-fragility, however, I have found that being comfortable in disorder is equally important, counteracting fragility with strength and resilience is valuable to build confidence, but so is living with fragility and using the countering force of levitas to create personal space in which to lead.

Whilst Covid-19 and the Twin Towers attacks of 9/11 are examples of more recent extreme black swans, some are more moderate. I am conscious that the distinction between moderate and extreme are very broad-brush labels and ultimately these depend on the interpretation and opinion of individuals. For example, when I first returned to London from Sydney I arrived at the start of the 2008 financial crisis. Some of the behaviors leading to the crisis had been created by many of the weaknesses of narcissists, the lack of gravitas by some business and political leaders to speak up and act when they knew the behaviors, particularly of large financial institutions, was deplorable and greedy. Non-Executive Directors (NEDs) who sat on the boards of numerous companies, across many sectors, with the remit to provide checks and balances to ensure that the behavior of leaders was appropriate, said nothing. Some NEDs were fearful to speak up, and at worst were simply there to collect their checks. Why did their many leaders' gravitas evaporate leading up to the crisis? Much of it stems from the motivation and underlying purpose of both individual leaders and the organizations they are a part of.

At a similar time I worked alongside a team tasked to help a global bank build a new culture to counter the behaviors that rocked the financial integrity of some institutions. One of the key components of creating this change culture was to understand their primary goals, motivation, and intent, and that meant addressing their core values. It's no good saying we wish to behave with more integrity and with values that reflect a caring world if the only motivator for the business and its leaders is simply to make money. And reinforced in a way where remuneration and bonuses are the only reflection of how performance is measured. You can imagine what their so-called authentic leadership looked like! Their website and annual report might have expressed their wider care for society and the environment, but nothing was going to change, and within a few months our team walked away. Developing their leaders' gravitas to lead in a volatile, uncertain, complex, and ambiguous world proved to be lip service because to them nothing unpredictable was going to happen again. Except that it did.

Some organizations operate in a culture of fear and often that is accompanied with leaders who felt a degree of 'imposter syndrome,' a personal sense of fraud and lack of worthiness. Not a financial sense of worth but one where leaders do not always feel they deserve to do what they do and one day they will be found out. I encountered some of this behavior when I was asked to assist a US investment firm. They wanted to build a more confident and open leadership culture where trust was at the center of their values, but in preparation I was warned by the human resources director of the firm that it was their performance culture that really defined how people related to one another. Each person felt they were being constantly assessed against one another but only on how they added financial value to the firm. They lived in fear that they simply were not good enough.

I've been in the company of senior executives learning that their company is being taken over, others facing the announcement of mass redundancies, stuck overseas when the Icelandic Eyjafjallajökull volcano erupted in 2010 with little chance of flying out for an undetermined time, and ultimately stuck in the UK when Covid-19 left me unable to get to the US to be with my partner for three months. Up until that point much of my work had required me or my clients to travel, but from that moment I was forced to rethink and figure out how to coach gravitas remotely. The idea of the workplace had taken a giant leap to somewhere we had not foreseen. All were versions of black swans.

When I am in a coaching environment it is easier to create a 'safe space' that enables clients to open up to their fragilities, than in a typical work space. And even though large group teaching environments are less conducive to individuals opening up, I always found that some individuals would seek me out for a private conversation about a fear, anxiety, phobia, or difficult relationship they are managing, often perceived as serious, creating an insurmountable barrier to their performance. However, rather than addressing these barriers as hurdles that they must overcome, I have found that reframing them where personal levity is more powerful or simply recognizing that being fragile is actually quite normal is much more effective. For many it is not the macro VUCA environment that poses the greatest situational leadership challenges, rather it is their micro environments of leading and relating to individuals with gravitas that proves most difficult, especially for introverts.

The magnetic tension between gravitas and levitas is almost a magical insight to building gravitas. A search of the meaning of levitas in Wiktionary (not available in other English dictionaries) reveals it as a noun defined as 'levity and lightness' but also as 'fickleness, volatility, shallowness and inconstancy.' I cannot imagine anyone wanting to have any of the last four attributed to their behavior, but they are nevertheless a reflection of the fragility of human behavior from time to time and the VUCA world in which we live. In the opening chapter to this book I introduced the five constructs of gravitas. Each of the constructs requires some levitas to ensure they are not overdone. The temperaments of being unflustered, being humble, finding balance, managing uncertainty, and adaptability are key levitas qualities for confidence, courage, credibility, control, and the communication constructs.

Later in the book I will introduce a tool to scan the environment and individuals to help understand whether you need more gravitas or levitas to have a greater impact, and we will learn about the impact of introverted and extroverted preferences to provide an insight into where your personal strengths and fragilities may lie.

Part Two

Reflecting

Chapter Four

Gravitas: Building a Picture

Earlier in the book I set out to explain what the roots of gravitas are and, in chapter one, provided a brief description of the five constructs and 21 temperaments that come together to define contemporary gravitas in leadership. I wanted to know whether gravitas is important, if so when is it important, and can it be developed. There is no point writing a book on the subject if the ultimate conclusion is 'nope,' you either have it or you don't.

So, let me first describe how I went about doing this because anyone can come up with a best guess about any of those questions, and for some that may be enough. However, two points: first, I have found that the more introverted often want to know where a form of thinking comes from to provide more depth; and second, I want to lay out how I approached it, so you can form your own opinion, comparing your ideas with mine. The reason why I explain this is part of knowing your gravitas and will require you to do some of your own research and reflective practice. Yep, you've got to work at it.

Before I really got stuck into behavioral science approaches, I did some groundwork asking a large sample of people about their opinions on the questions I first laid out, which I will also ask you to do in a later chapter, but for now you may simply want to journal some notes on your thoughts to each question. Drawing on my close network and subsequently an extended network I was able to survey engineers, teachers, students, doctors, academics, board members, contract lawyers, and actors just to name a few professions. I aimed to achieve a pretty even gender split, and the key questions I asked were:

1. What do you understand by the term gravitas?
2. How do you know when someone has this quality?
3. Who have you come across who you regard as having gravitas?
4. What effect did those people have on you?
5. Do you believe someone can acquire gravitas and how?
6. How are presence and charisma both similar and different?
7. In what contexts is gravitas important?
8. What are the barriers to gravitas?

You'll be able to reflect on these later in greater depth or no doubt you already are. Based on responses it seemed to me that gravitas is a quality of the person as a whole, inwardly and outwardly. It has authenticity, certainly, however, being authentic appeared insufficient because if the outwardly displayed actions and thoughts do not reflect the inner beliefs, it is not gravitas. Many people can be authentic but when that person cannot engage others, does not have traits that attract others, does not have substance to add weight when needed to situations, and does not have integrity, all the authenticity in the world is not enough.

I also deduced that people felt that gravitas added value to others when it is helpful, and were confident enough to form opinions that others find interesting even if others may not agree but do so in such a way that is open and balanced. In a way my intuition sensed that gravitas could be passed on to others. The somatic embodiment of gravitas seemed to be critical, and raised the question that although the body will often follow the mind, can we develop the embodiment of gravitas to influence the mind? This proved to be important, as we shall practice in the third part on "Performing."

When asked about people they perceived as having gravitas understandably I was thrown names of people that they hadn't necessarily met. What I could deduce is that there is not a one size fits all type of person. The idea of a body and mind in balance with itself was often accepted, and a sense of calmness coupled with humility appeared to be very important. The connection with a calm humility fostered my first thoughts that levity was equally important to any sense of gravity.

Two of the last four questions were so important, asking whether one can acquire and develop gravitas, and how and what sort of barriers tended to be obstructive. Some people I met early on in my efforts to teach and coach gravitas believed it to be an elusive and unteachable quality. If everyone had agreed there would be no wiggle room at all. Fortunately for all of us, most people asked said it was possible, including nearly all of my students and participants. Often there were some caveats such as, "yes ... but it depends on the type of education you had, yes ... if you have certain traits and so on." I am all too aware, though, that a lot people would hope and want it to be achievable. After all a completely elusive quality doesn't inspire us much.

I learned that it was important to step out of our comfort zone and meet new people, even if it is something you tend to avoid, because it will be a valuable learning experience. Also, ensure that one combines reflective self-awareness practices, and learning what you are good at and passionate about; find a purpose and become a sponge at all times! Some aspects of coaching, education, and training are important and often a great opportunity to build self-awareness, but ultimately, observation, self-reflection, and real world practice as a constant cycle of personal growth are what helps us to find our gravitas. There isn't a quick fix and we should be happy about that, but there are adjustments physically and mentally that can help rescue gravitas in the moment. However, true inner gravitas takes time and requires effort.

People who were seen to be negative or overly use negative language were perceived as lacking gravitas, and also having attitudes that would hinder them personally. Nevertheless, not listening, not understanding, not seeing, and not having something gives us a window of opportunity. It gives us a chance to have something, but it will need work as these behaviors, habits, and attitudes have been honed over many years. Whilst youth might have been tabled as a barrier by some I questioned it also is something that can be a benefit when change is needed. Where experience was tabled as a benefit, it also presents a greater barrier when we need to adapt something that is so ingrained. So, let's reflect on these barriers a little more.

Over the 30+ years I have been teaching and coaching, the number one barrier I have faced is cynicism. Cynics or skeptics can be a useful sanity check at times and so often come from those voices with significant experience and subject matter expertise, but they also look for reasons not to try something new. I heard from my sample and students that gravitas in a business setting was often most important during periods of change as I described in the previous chapter. Not only did this affect business leaders that were part of my research but many of the professions that reflected my sample. Therefore, in this context of dramatic global change gravitas is proving not just a desirable quality, but an essential one.

Negativity might be a sibling of cynicism, but I have found it to be an overarching attitude that permeates all aspects of life. Therefore, my opening point on making personal changes here is to find the positive in situations and others, and find a way to make ourselves and our ideas relevant to others. A common theme I have found in coaching introverted senior people in business is that they often find it difficult to engage with others. Taking a dive into what that means is that they can find it difficult to empathize, difficult to do small talk, can't articulate, can't find the lightness and humility that appeals to many, and carry self-doubt about their abilities. That is quite a list undoubtedly, but all of us will have met one or more of these barriers at some time. On an optimistic point these are the very types of people and situations that can benefit the most from learning how to develop gravitas and levitas. These are my favorite people because despite their worries they tend to be the most knowledge hungry. For example, on one course I was working for a week with senior engineers in a well-known global company. Each of them led others, departments, functions, and businesses. On one occasion I was working with one such engineer, and having worked through a series of exercises over the first two days to build self-awareness he declared to me, "Ian, I prefer to see myself as a machine. It's much easier to be a machine. I don't have to think about emotions and feelings and usually won't get things wrong." "Interesting," I replied. "Unfortunately, human beings are not machines, so I wonder how does being a machine being work out for you?" "Not well," he replied. "The problem I see is that the people I work with don't think they are machines." My initial thought was, oh dear this is going to be tough, but as I was speaking with him, I thought, here he is sharing this in front of a group of peers. That takes courage. It also demonstrated self-awareness and a clue that he might be interested in learning more. That was the beautiful thing. He was an ideal person on which develop and test ideas. The opposite type of person is the worst by far.

Those with no interest in others, living through their self-absorbed ego, and pride, and have no interest in listening to others are the closed-off narcissists of the world. They believe they are right and always look for others to celebrate them, and expect a loyalty and undying devotion to them. Do you have any ideas of people like this? I'm sure you do. If you are one of these people, this book is not for you. As we shall explore later you need to be careful to ensure you are not using narcissists as role models. It will not work. They do not have gravitas, but they will be the first to say they do.

Developing the Architecture

If you can't explain it simply you simply don't understand it.
– Albert Einstein

Academics, engineers, even artists love a model. I'm none of those really but as a practitioner educator, mentor, and coach I am also drawn to a model. It creates a simple visual image to hold in the mind, and once probed in a multidimensional sense, it allows one to test its applicability and depth of understanding. So, when I had considered the responses from those early questionnaires and reflected on my one-to-one interviews and 20+ years of coaching, I began to draft what a model might look like.

I hoped that I could find some type of single gravitas formula ensuring it was based on my research experiences. However, I was finding gravitas had many layers of complexity due to our unique personalities, and would need to reflect how important it was for people to adapt to situations quickly. It was in a sense a series of three-dimensional formulae that would change with any situation.

For example, communication is the fifth ranking construct, but I believe it needs to be underpinned by a high degree of self-confidence, and backed up with credibility in the eyes of the followers. Confidence is observed, heard, felt, and experienced by others. It is also infectious. It is in part derived by a level of self-belief, reinforced by experience and comfort with the situational context. Confidence is a complex personal psychological state but in the context of gravitas it is also a requirement that it is instilled in others. It was also difficult in my experience to have gravitas without credibility. Credibility may be earned or apparent. Where it is earned, there are experiences to draw on and wisdom to share. If it was apparent, others could visually see a perceived credibility and, together with confidence, this could be embodied so that it was visually and emotionally apparent to others. Control conceived from my understanding of leadership as an ability to influence others (Yukl, 2002; Bass and Bass, 2008). Rather than use the word influence, I decided to use the word control because I felt it would be easier to remember labels beginning with the same letter. I also felt that it had the advantage of reflecting the inner control of the alignment of moods and values to outer expression (Avolio and Gardner, 2005; Harter, 2002; Erickson, 1995).

The following image shows the initial grid model I worked from and a simple scale from low to high across four axes. What I was trying to convey was not whether one had or did not have gravitas, but a shift towards a concept of differing amounts of situational gravitas in the same way that Erickson (1995) referred to achieving levels of authenticity. At the back of my mind was always the question, why does my gravitas evaporate in certain situations?

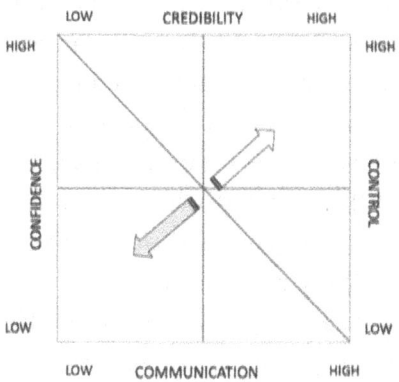

Figure 4.1: The four quadrants of gravitas.

Having initially concluded that there isn't one gravitas description, equation, or formula, I realized somehow that I would need a way to allow individuals to describe it for themselves and to assess where they needed to focus when their gravitas was under threat.

So, I turned to a method called the 'conceptual encounter' because it makes it specific to you. The reason I introduce it in the book is that I will ask you to use an adapted version of it in the assessment of your own gravitas. The key question I began with is almost philosophical — whether gravitas is 'real' or not. It's just a word after all, isn't it? We know for example that unicorns do not exist, but if you were to ask a child to draw a unicorn they could do so with little hesitation. Once we introduce a language to describe something it has a form of reality just like many other things do if you think about it, and the conceptual encounter method is a way of coloring in a word in such a way that describes a quality or an emotion in enough detail that it makes sense to anyone but especially to you.

Dr. Joseph de Rivera pioneered the approach to understand human experience of emotions such as love or anger, and conditions such as anxiety. If you think about it, anger is felt and expressed differently by each of us, and our reaction is also dependent on the people we encounter. Gravitas is the same. The situation we encounter added to our reaction inside, and how we outwardly project ourselves, and then how it is perceived by others dictates our gravitas. We don't need to have gravitas all the time but when we need it, it is essential. However, it's alarming that when we often need it the most we may ask, where did my gravitas go?

The conceptual encounter method provides a technique to map the experiences of humans to a specific emotion. Within the approach there are certain processes that are known as 'looking rules' enabling a systematic deep inspection into the experience so that it becomes recognizable not only to the person or persons being explored, but also to others.

There are parallels between the conceptual encounter method's aim to create simple and elegant explanations and the physicists' or mathematicians' ideas of universal laws. Professor Brian Cox states in his book, *Human Universe*, that Henry Cavendish's experiment in 1797–1798, the first to measure the force of gravity between the masses to find a gravitational constant, is a "brilliant simplification," stating the "quest for elegance and economy guides physicists to this day." Whilst the quest for a unifying single explanation for the universe continues Professor Stephen Hawking wrote in his hugely educational and entertaining book, *A Brief History in Time*, "we now know it is impossible to have an infinite static model of the universe in which gravity is always attractive." In some ways it also reminds me of the often-told quote from Winston Churchill when invited to give a speech at his alma mater Oxford University:

> if you want me to speak for two minutes, it will take me three weeks of preparation, if you want me to speak for thirty minutes it will take me one week to prepare, if you want me to speak for one hour, I am ready now.

As a result, therefore, I wanted an image and framework that was simple enough to capture gravitas and room to dig deeper so that it could bend and flex enough to personalize it for everyone. It, like the universe, is not static.

Let me share with you some of the stories and responses from just a few of the leaders I got to know well as they explained gravitas to me through a series of evolving interviews.

An Emerging Framework of Gravitas

Rick (not his real name) was an engineer, had been managing teams for around 15 years, and was probably in the second half of his career. When I asked him what he perceived as the most distinguishing feature of gravitas, he stated:

> For me, it boils right down to the person who says the most but while saying the least ... because I always try and think these things down to the simplest thing and you just don't have to talk all the time or be the loudest but that when you do speak, your voice is the loudest.

The area of authenticity was interesting to Rick as he suggested that sometimes his gravitas was reduced if he was being authentic. He explained that in some cases being authentic meant saying he did not like a particular person or situation, but that it would be unhelpful or damaging or unacceptable in his organization.

I spent many weeks with Danielle (not her real name) trying to build on my framework and challenge any views that others had expressed. There was far more time spent discussing where confidence emerges for her, how she had to prove to herself she deserved to be where she was, and how she tried to convey gravitas to herself and others. The most significant difference I found was that she related gravitas to warmth and approachability, and not with Rick's view on being right or correct when leading. I also found that Rick had related more of his experiences to him feeling as though he had gravitas, but with Danielle she observed it more often in other people.

Rebecca was younger than Rick and Danielle, and she associated gravitas strongly with confidence and communication. Her description of experiences was similar to Danielle's in relation to her need to convey confidence, especially to men, and she felt a lot of the perception of confidence would come through the way she communicated. A similarity with Danielle was that she also described it in others rather than herself.

John was one of my deep thinker partners and on a fast track to a top leadership role. He had been a high achiever all his life in work and education, and also been mentored by one of the top people in his company. He told me gravitas was an experience one felt, and although there was a physicality to it especially when observing others, no matter who you were you could develop gravitas through a coached and mentored approach. He was more fascinated with the need to control situations and not let them control you, and as such needed an ability to scan and adapt quickly to situations.

Mike, a very charismatic leader, saw gravitas as a more personal set of skills and qualities, slightly at odds to John. He was drawn more to magnetic quality, a person with depth, and was quite clear in his mind that it was related to a deeper relational approach built over time that connects one to another. In contrast he emphasized he felt that presence was a feeling in the moment, which echoed my feeling about the difference between presence and gravitas.

Another of my partners was Kirsty, and I noticed that some of her thoughts clearly matched some of those of the other women I had spent time interviewing. She described where she became frustrated at not having sufficient self-belief to lead, and wanted gravitas to help build real confidence and her self-belief. She also strongly associated gravitas with warmth and approachability. The constructs of confidence and credibility seemed to be more important to the women than to the men. However, everyone I worked with agreed they were key constructs of gravitas.

These only represent a few of the interview responses that I have conducted over many years, and it is clear how personal and individual their perceptions are. During a research phase for every single key leader I focused on, I also interviewed those that worked for them, their peers, the person they reported to, and indeed a few at the very top level. It's slow and painfully detailed work as every conversation is recorded, listened to over and over again, transcribed, reanalyzed, coded, themed, and summarized. It's not particularly enjoyable but as patterns emerge, the choice of language and examples are extremely satisfying when you get to an end point. The detailed descriptions gleaned from all of my encounters helped to explain each major theme heading, rather like the building blocks of DNA sequencing. Ultimately as you digest my description and model of gravitas you are invited to do what I would expect you to do anyway. Weigh up what you think and then add, subtract, or reaffirm the constructs based on your experiences.

Chapter Five

Understanding the Constructs of Gravitas

Let's summarize where we have got to so far. Every person's understanding of gravitas is slightly different depending on their core qualities and weaknesses. There is an overlapping between the constructs and the DNA of each construct called temperaments, that when combined build an overall strength of gravitas. All of those whom I drew from their experiences in leadership roles described how difficult it can be to build credibility and confidence with more senior leaders than themselves, but also how important it was to do so. I discovered through working with the most senior leaders what they wanted to see in gravitas from more junior level leaders was more courage and to be prepared to speak their mind. However, this was not simple once an organization's culture was taken into account, and as one CEO emphasized to me, they also believed it was the job of the most senior personnel to instill courage and confidence in others, so they felt enabled to speak their minds. In so doing they injected a positivity in others that created a type of 'micro climate' which encourages others to act. So, gravitas is not only projected, it must be received and passed on to others.

The addition of courage as another construct was a significant evolution of my model, and it actually is the central hub around which the other constructs rotate. Gravitas requires an individual to take a risk and that sets them apart from others. In so doing it exposes a personal vulnerability or fragility which requires an inner strength of character. I also learned how gravitas really is distinguished from authentic and charismatic leadership. Gravitas is a quality of the person and a perception of others. There is an inward and outward gravitas. It is a felt quality from within firstly, whereas authenticity and charisma are defined primarily through the perception of others.

The balance between finding a parsimonious framework and the complexity of the construct markers meant that I needed a way of graphically representing the concept. I had started with more of a cube, but it felt too rigid and static. I also had built a sphere combining circles of shields, but as enjoyable as it was trying to find the right image I ultimately chose something much simpler. A propeller.

The propeller is made up of four blade faces with a central hub. Moving together they create a force, an energy which provides thrust. Just as I imagine the force of gravitas is. As I wrote earlier, the hub which the others revolve around turned out to be the last of the key constructs that I found, courage.

Let's take a look at the constructs and in some more detail.

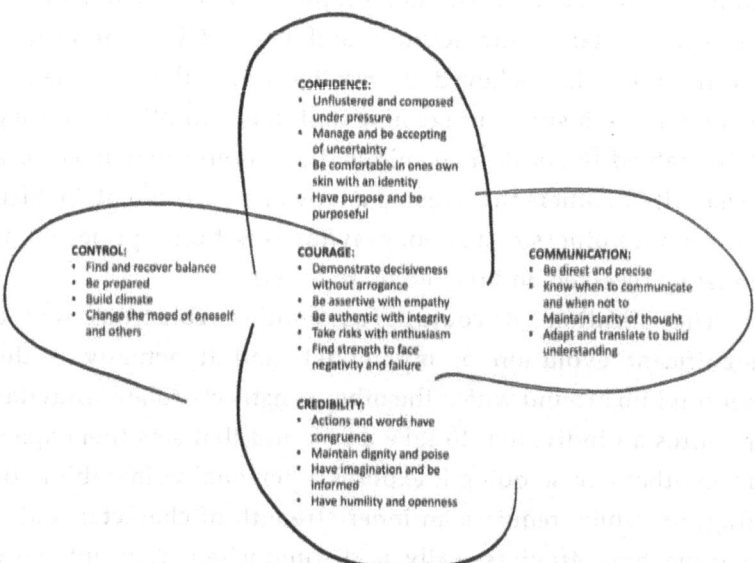

Figure 5.1: The 'propeller blade' model of Gravitas

Exploring Each Construct through the Temperaments
Courage

Fear is a reaction, courage is a decision.
— Sir Winston Churchill

Ernest Hemingway once said, "courage is grace under pressure." There is something both stylistic and action focused about courage. It may be the last construct to have joined the other four, but it is at the center of gravitas; to have gravitas requires courage first. There is both a moral and physical dimension — to have the conviction to act or to do what you feel is right. The courage of your convictions in spite of what others may think, in spite of opposition, negativity, or criticism. And in some cases, a somatic courage in the face of physical threat or danger. In 'old' English it is described as "valor, a quality of mind and ability to face danger without fear" (etymonline.com). The root of the word takes us to the Latin and French meaning for the word 'cor' or couer, meaning 'of the heart,' rather like the lion from 1939 film *The Wizard of Oz*, in search of his courage.

Perhaps the idea of facing danger with no fear is a little unrealistic. If you're faced with someone holding a gun to your head or find yourself face to face with a lion you will hardly be fearless. It is also quite likely that you wouldn't have access to courage, but the brain and the mind will become entirely focused or even frozen on survival. To some extent that part of the brain I discussed earlier which is entirely instinctive can work against us. Our brain can begin to over process. I will cover the management of anxiety and panic later but even before those heightened states fear can be obstructive to our development. I have no intention of addressing the nature of fear in any detail here. For that I would again point you in the direction of Susan Jeffers' excellent book, *Feel the Fear and Do*

It Anyway. But fear can create an unhelpful setting in the mind that translates that fear into worry, passiveness, negativity, and paralysis. A type of 'learned helplessness' emerges and it tends to build. Fear of something that needs to be faced escalates over time as nothing is done, and time passes by until it eats us up. It might be a personal financial issue, a people problem, a work or study project that is heading nowhere, a fear of social settings, or even a personal nagging of self-doubt (inferiority complex) of our own abilities. I identified five key temperaments for courage.

As with all of the temperaments of courage I found there to be paradoxes. To be X without being Y. And so, Hemingway's description of grace under severe pressure is not necessarily a natural state. Our neurotransmitters plot against us, and when courage is needed it is always when there is a degree of pressure.

We all make decisions every day but very few require much conscious processing. However, being decisive is somewhat different. So, what is being decisive? The main two characteristics are that decisions are made quickly and effectively. To be effective is to gain the results one intended. To do so quickly is sometimes at the cost of not always having all the facts needed but enough experience and instinct to ensure the outcome intended. Again, it is about managing the paradox of sufficient time and gathering of the facts. It often is accompanied by moments of crisis and is a distinguishing feature of leadership. Fortunately, moments of crisis for many are not daily features of life. However, in some professions, for example the military, first responders, pilots, even teachers, especially in the USA with such high levels of gun crime, training and practice help to ensure that when real crises occur there is a degree of automated response to be decisive. The other face of decisiveness is in the face of resistance, and this is where most of us will be tested. Here it is not so much speed of the decision-making but rather finding a way to navigate those that do not agree with us. Riding over them as I described earlier depletes our gravitas and may make us seen as arrogant.

Undoubtedly there is crossover between the constructs of confidence, communication, and control within the temperament of assertiveness because it requires one to communicate, control of the self, both body and mind, and the courage to be yourself. The balancing act again is really delicate here but actually not difficult to master. Some types of personalities find it more difficult to be assertive regardless of whether it is with empathy or without. For example, introverts with considerable shyness simply will sometimes choose to avoid being assertive when it is required face to face whether in person or on screen. They may be comfortable in the written form, but as we will see when we move to the tactics to deploy, there are cultural, both national and organizational, that sometimes cause confusion and frustration when relying upon. Equally, however, the energy of the extrovert can be overpowering and as a result lack the intended gravitas needed to be attractive to others.

I devoted a whole section earlier to authenticity as there has been so much written about it. However, finding your own authenticity has a very strong link to the confidence temperament of being comfortable with your identity. A lot of the activities in the gravitas self-assessment chapter examine our level of self-awareness, and we have learned that it is a mixture of inner self-knowledge and how others see our integrity. Often, it's only a perception but when allied to the credibility temperament of congruence with actions and words it moves beyond perception to actuality. Becoming more a nature of trust than the ability to build authentic relationships. I'm not usually a fan of x+y=z with human behavior but I have one exception: the trust equation. It was first written about by David Maister in 2000, and in his book, he describes trust as a combination of Credibility (C) + Reliability (R) + Intimacy (I) divided by Self Orientation (S) = Trust. Credibility is already one of our constructs, but reliability also features as a part of congruence. It really means doing what we say we are going to do, added to by our ability to build relationships (intimacy) which is diluted if the focus of our intentions is always ourselves (S). The ugly narcissist trait brought up earlier. Another way of using a different lens to consider our own authenticity is to ask yourself, when are you or have you been inauthentic?

Risk taking is undoubtedly a courageous act; as Winston Churchill is believed to have suggested, fear is a reaction, but courage is a decision. Some people by their own nature are risk adverse. It doesn't have to be anything to do with life risking situations. For some a risk is simply to speak to someone at a party or to talk in front of a group. It is a very personal temperament and requires an inner strength to face the consequences of how you might feel after taking that risk. Strength is a temperament learned by reinforcement, and our attitude towards introversion and extroversion. Our exposure to risk and reinforcement as children can help to define our reaction but also just recognizing that our inner critic can be quietened down as we will explore in the section on coaching ourselves. Introverts are naturally more inclined to self-judgement but also good at inner processing and revaluation. Extroverts are sometimes seen as thicker skinned, but I haven't found that to be the case. They find their strength from reframing situations, and focus on what's next.

Confidence

Confidence is a construct that appears to ebb and flow far more than the other four. Situationally our confidence is always being stretched from one end to another, and is one of the key constructs I will focus on in the tactics and strategies chapter in order to help read situations quickly. We cannot be confident all the time, fortunately. We can coach ourselves into various emotional states quickly, but they can leave us just as quickly. Unfortunately, it is the negative emotional states that tend to stick around. Once we begin to tell ourselves we are not good enough or we are going to fail we start to look for reinforcing information to support our argument. The whole construct has a strong relationship between the temperament of finding and recovering balance in the construct of control.

The ebb and flow are captured somewhat in the self-assessment where we have an opportunity to say if we have too little of a confidence temperament or too much, but that will only capture our best guess in general without attaching it to a moment in time. What we will need is a set of skills to work with the temperaments when we need to. Confidence isn't required all of the time but knowing how to access yours makes life easier. Most people going to the supermarket, for example, don't require any confidence building, but actually for some it does. Those with a fear of outdoor spaces (agoraphobia) are terrified and will avoid it at all costs. One of my stepsons often needs to have his confidence built to go somewhere to shop for something, especially if he doesn't know where it is and if he ever needs to ask for help in the store. This isn't uncommon. People sometimes fear asking others for help, getting directions, asking an expert for help, or seeing a medical doctor, and so on. What we will need to do is identify the situations where our temperaments are at risk and which ones matter. Remember also that every time we think of working on one of our temperaments we may need to help instill the same in others. We will return to why that is important. As a clue it has a strong link to equaling the gravitational force of others — as in equaling the mass of another.

Being unflustered was such a popular idea with most people I have worked with, and although we landed on being unflustered and composed, others referred to it as simply being calm. However, calm was a little too passive. We will work with imagery techniques with many of the temperaments, and they work well with this temperament especially. To manage and be accepting of uncertainty is a mental shift we have all made in the last few years, and was discussed in the chapter describing environmental volatility. But it is also a real temperament. It often helps to look at ourselves as if we are an observer viewing our unflusteredness from the outside, teaching us to slow down and learning to accept we can't always be right or know what is going to happen. We have to use our judgement, listening and absorbing information, and recognize how we can learn from the unintended consequences of our actions.

Being comfortable is the third temperament I really like, when it is attached to the idea of being comfortable 'in our own skin and identity.' It grew in meaning. On one hand, when my research found how many people describe seeing confident people as looking comfortable, it immediately takes a somatic direction. Fortunately, somatic comfort is quick to work with, but developing an identity and feeling comfortable inside is much slower. When I have worked with people who describe themselves as shy they often also describe feeling uncomfortable. However, working with shy people is actually a really enjoyable area of work because the impact on using shyness and identity is very powerful. What tends to happen is that certain types of people make shy people really uncomfortable. Once we learn how to identify them, a shy person can use a strength they don't even know they have to really stand out, in a way that doesn't hurt. It requires a determination and willingness to step out of our safe comfort zone.

The last temperament, having a purpose and being purposeful, like authenticity is a popular subject. If you enter an Amazon search for 'purpose' in the books section you will find hundreds on the topic, albeit not in this context. But even so there is an appeal to finding purpose. It provides direction and a reason for being. We will use some examples in the tactics chapter to help frame a way of thinking, but more importantly we will need to ensure that we are purposeful and consistent with bringing that purpose to life; communicating with it and having the courage to stand by it.

Credibility

The true sign of intelligence is not knowledge but imagination.
— Albert Einstein

Earlier I distinguished between apparent and earned credibility. But there is more than that. There is as much substance to the feeling of credibility as there is of it being genuinely earned. In the next chapter I bring up a brief history of some of the founding thinkers on how we develop psychologically. But for now as a means of introducing some barriers to credibility I'll refer to Alfred Adler's description of two psychological states, inferiority complex and perhaps the lesser known superiority complex. I have worked with those who would acknowledge that they suffer from symptoms associated with imposter syndrome, and often discovered that how others feel about them can be quite at odds with their own perceptions. Incidentally imposter syndrome does tend to be situational and more of a work-based challenge where inferiority complex can permeate in all parts of life and poses the greater barrier. We will get to some of the important self-development work in the self-assessment chapter but before we get there start to consider — how would others describe you? Believe it or not there are some people who will answer that in a machine almost computer-like fashion — height, eye color, hair color etc. Yes, they really do. Maybe you would! But how others describe you under the construct of credibility is interesting as it shows the consistency or lack of it in terms of our behavior and our actions.

Our 'leadership shadow' compares four areas: what we say, how we act, what we measure, and what we prioritize as a guidance on how congruent we are. We could add to 'how we act' how we appear — our poise and dignity. One of my early respondents when asked when gravitas was important provided a three-word reply. At a funeral. I couldn't argue with that. There is a physicality to credibility just as there is to all the constructs but with credibility it is quickly lost under pressure. The last two temperaments of credibility are wonderful. Firstly, to have imagination and be informed. Albert Einstein described it as far more important than knowledge. My former English teacher must have agreed and wrote in one of my school reports: "Ian has a great capacity for staring out of the window!" On reflection, decades later I hoped she meant that I had imagination, but I doubt it. There needs to be a balance between being informed, open-minded and learning from others and testing that with imagination. Being credible means being interested in others. It's the 'I' from the trust equation and dovetails equally with the last temperament of humility and openness. Humility and imagination especially provide the levitas in gravitas. All that weight of being credible needs to get off the ground.

Control

I can't quite remember when I wrote my own notes for a course on gravitas, but I recall at one point drawing a series of pictures of a 'Sensei' teaching a student in a martial art. And I also recall that I had recently been on a course for a few days led by a group of Shaolin monks. That in itself might pique your interest, but what made it unique, is that it was done without any speaking. We spent most of the first day attempting to meditate. I have learnt more about meditating since then but at the time, about 15 or more years ago, it was one of my first experiences. But back to the course. Have you ever or would you ever attend a course in silence for four days? We were taught to communicate using shapes, images of animals, and copying their behavior or responding to their movements in basic martial arts techniques.

It was fascinating, but I always remember that there was a series of exercises about finding and recovering balance. I loved it, and the idea of bouncing back physically and mentally.

When we lose our balance, we are unstable. There is no gravitas, no weight, with instability. If we can teach our troubled and stressed mind to recover we begin to take control. If possible, we can maintain control of ourselves through being prepared. Every activity in the tactics chapter will need practice so as to be prepared. Dale Carnegie once wrote in his famous book, *How to Develop Self Confidence and Improve Public Speaking*, that one of the essential elements is to be prepared. I think it gives us control as much as it does contribute to confidence. You tend to need gravitas in the presence of others. You hardly look in the mirror and announce, "I've got gravitas!" You need it under pressure. That's why it tends to go. If preparation and practice (mentally or otherwise) improve control of yourself, you have a much better chance at influencing others. Building climate is the third temperament and I think it is essential in the company of others. How you look, move, think, act, and speak changes the climate but it's also a product of intention. Therefore, you can choose the climate around you if you wish to influence it. As a teacher and professor, I have always been aware that this is probably the number one goal when I lead a room. I will show you how to do it soon, but even if the climate does shift unintentionally you need to know how to make sure your mood does not shift negatively and change the mood of others, especially when working with disruptive or toxic influences.

Communication

Tact is the ability to tell someone to go to hell in such a way that they look forward to the trip.

— Sir Winston Churchill

The final construct of gravitas, communication, is hardly surprising. Every book I have read on a similar subject has a heavy emphasis on communication, and so much of my coaching work before being asked to exclusively focus on gravitas was communicating. It is the direct link we have to others, and it is not always spoken of course. There are a lot of cultural considerations to take into account in this area. For example, when I moved from England to Australia, my Scottish new boss warned me about not appearing to be arrogant. I quizzed him, and he said all the British sound arrogant to the Australian ear when they first arrive. Equally when I ran psychometric testing in Japan, Indonesia, Singapore, and South Korea, there were huge variances in each of those countries about whether they should answer questions that supported what their boss would say or be free to answer how they might want to if it was different. In Northern Scandinavia and Eastern Europe, the idea of being more expressive and smiling more was at odds with the perception of communicating with gravitas. Even when I moved from the UK to the USA there were huge communication gaps. Not the words exactly but the choice of how much to say. This translated into the style of communication in both the written form and the spoken word. In the US I found written communication to be shorter and more abrupt. Whenever my American wife had to write an email to a client or colleague in the UK she would ask me to read through the overall style. And for some reason I felt the need to 'pad' it out. My language was a little bit more 'flowery,' something my Russian doctoral supervisor used to abhor and tried to train out of me. In turn, however, both my wife and supervisor taught me to be more direct and offer a more edited style of written and verbal communication. There isn't a right or wrong way to write but becoming conscious of your own style and working through how to adapt and translate it for different cultures and different audiences is essential.

The temperament of being direct and precise is to be used carefully. Situations where gravitas is needed normally has extra pressure where careful editing of our words is essential. Less often equals more in those instances, however, when dealing with personal issues, perhaps the opposite is needed. It is all a question of reading the situation. Knowing when and when not to communicate is equally delicate. The earlier example of attending a work social function is a case in point. It will be hard to have gravitas without speaking at all, but what do you say if you have a fear of 'small talk'? Part of the skill comes from the last two temperaments: maintaining clarity of thought, and adapting and translating for those listening. I will address these specifically in the chapter on tactics but also teach the somatic skills that help to clear the mind and relax our physiology.

Chapter Six

Knowing Your Gravitas

Knowing yourself is the beginning of all wisdom.
— Aristotle

When you want to build a picture of your own gravitas you need to obtain an understanding of the differences between how you are now compared against the 21 gravitas temperaments and where you might like to be. Bearing in mind of course that it is not a static comparison as situations change constantly and we react with them. But the starting point is always to gauge a level of self-awareness that fits with a comfortable balance between self-perception and how others see us.

Due to the nature of my work there have been very few courses I have led or been a part of where some degree of self-awareness and assessment hasn't taken place. Sometimes they centered around the use of a particular behavioral measurement tool or instrument, sometimes a psychodynamic activity, or both. We will get to psychodynamics shortly. However, even when the overall focus of a course might be, for example, strategy, or finance, managing change, building a brand, or innovation and entrepreneurship and so on, ultimately, they often begin and end with personal development through awareness, growth, and practice, and for most it becomes the most meaningful investment of their time. Time and again a client would spend a huge amount of money sending their employees away for a few days (often 20% or so overseas) and then spend half of it with their own senior executives rolling up to present an overused set of 'in house' presentations and explore a range of topics that they already knew about before, and everyone breathing a sigh of relief when they left and we could all get on with what was most valuable!

One of the few benefits of the Covid-19 impact on traditional working locations and roles has been that there is not the same level of demand for face-to-face group courses and a reevaluation of what really makes a difference to personal performance. The challenge though for those seeking to build and understand gravitas is that the range of theaters in which our performance takes place is more complex, and the nature of gravitas and our development is also more complex. For some personalities this period is an immense opportunity to work in different contexts which we will cover next.

As a doctor of coaching and mentoring psychology it's perhaps unsurprising that I have always loved using 'psych' tools alongside self-reflection activities for self-awareness practice. I am all too aware, however, that some of my former adult students have been either suspicious or outright dismissive of their ability to provide a picture or description of them. I'll address the pros and cons alongside my preferences for which activities work the best, and dovetail these with a series of gravitas assessment exercises before we start on the tactics and strategies for working with the gravitas temperaments in life.

Let's consider the options available as a step one for building self-awareness. Psychometric tests or assessments are a good starting point for gravitas awareness. In general, they fall into three categories, as either assessments of ability or aptitude, capabilities and preferred behaviors, or personality. I began first using tests of verbal and numerical reasoning nearly 30 years ago when I worked in full-time teaching and college lecturing, but my first exposure to psychometric assessment for working adults was around five years later using the DISC instrument. It is a behavioral assessment tool that often people believe describes four personality types: dominance, influence, steadiness, and conscientiousness. It is used to help understand

and improve performance in the workplace, and like any tool it has its limitations. The first I have pointed out really is that many people believe it is a personality assessment and it isn't. It describes the kind of behavior a person tends to orientate to in the workplace in a relatively simplistic two-dimensional way, and captures the person's thinking at the time when they complete the questionnaire. As a self-awareness tool, it is too restrictive for this book. But what I want to raise is that for many who might read this you have probably already completed some types of assessments, and it is useful to understand which ones might help and those that may not. However, if it's all you have available at this time it can still be a useful starting point.

The FIRO-B assessment tool is an excellent tool for coaching, including working with your inner coach. It was originally designed in the 1950s to help improve the performance of teams. Particularly teams that work under pressure, and in this instance began with submarine teams with their own obvious situational and environmental pressures. It is somewhat unique as it looks at how we express ourselves outwardly but also what we expect or would like to receive back. It is excellent as an interrelational tool, but I believe works best when working with an external coach. I would suggest it particularly if the reader is purely using this book from a work role performance improvement angle, however, in my experience with gravitas, there is a desire for people to find theirs in all aspects of their lives and therefore would look to an instrument which is easier to understand, and many will have used before: the Myers-Briggs Type Indicator.

Gravitas Assessment: The Myers-Briggs Type Indicator®

> *The world will ask who you are and if you don't know the world will tell you.*
>
> *– Carl Jung*

I first qualified in the use of what is abbreviated as the MBTI (Myers-Briggs Type Indicator) in 1998, at the request of the human resources director of a car company (manufacturer not dealer) when I took on my first commercial management role after leaving my job as a Senior Lecturer in higher education. The company had previously relied on the aforementioned DISC for recruitment and development purposes. I have never been keen on any instruments as recruitment or classification methods (I'm thinking of university candidate tools as well) for three reasons. Firstly, the bias of the recruiter or otherwise senior role; secondly because for many, the process of completing a test or assessment is inherently stressful; and thirdly, it only captures that moment in time. The third issue is the most important. They are not suitable to classify individuals for roles. Individuals adapt and use their strengths and modify supposed weaker sides and it should really be a question of character and capability. Many years ago (1980s) as a former Royal Air Force military young chap I attended something called OASC. Officer and Aircrew Selection Centre at Biggin Hill, a former WWII 'Battle of Britain' fighter command station. The selection process took a number of days and was a shock to a young civilian. All that shouting, rigorous addiction to precise time, and sharing space with strangers. If any of you have been through anything similar you will know the feeling well, maybe even fondly with time! Anyway, the recruitment process, although it includes a number of 'tests,' focuses on what we now call experiential activities and 'in the moment' tests of character. It isn't perfect, but it tries to allow the candidate to 'perform' over time. Obviously, it is guided by the ideal of a perfect type of military candidate to mold, but it is more useful than a quick test to whittle down a group of people for a single job. And therefore, I am not a fan of psychometrics as tools for recruitment. However, when my ex-army tank commanding human resources director asked me to qualify as an MBTI practitioner, at the time, I was a huge fan. It sounded like something with real depth and of course would add another dimension to my young career. He had wanted me to use it primarily as a recruitment instrument and secondly as a development tool, but after my few days away in Oxford, UK, on a thoroughly enjoyable course, I learned quickly that it would be an immoral recruitment tool and really not an assessment of personality. However, it was eye-opening as a self-awareness and development instrument. I loved it. I stopped it being used as a recruitment tool almost immediately, but it needs some explanation because I am going to recommend it highly as a first step in gravitas self-assessment and fortunately it can be completed online.

I had initially studied psychology as part of my first degree, but as interesting as the mind is it is hard not to have an interest in both the mind and the body which was what I was most interested in after leaving the air force. I had played tennis in the Royal Air Force and then at Carnegie Sports and Education Faculty within Leeds Metropolitan University, and was also exposed to many other sports too. Not that I played well, but hopefully very enthusiastically. As a student within the Carnegie faculty we mostly wore the Carnegie track suits to university so as to distinguish us from the rest. My younger brother was one of the rest and pretty much ridiculed us both for our Carnegie gang mentality and PE teacher in waiting careers. But in my world, I loved it. Sport, leisure, a bit of sociology and psychology thrown in. It didn't qualify me for much, but I enjoyed learning and did find a career teaching what I'd learnt, and later as a college professor with a few more degrees thrown in. But what I never did lose was a fascination with how the mind and body work. So, fast forward to a middle management job in a car company learning to use MBTI and I started to find a little bit of direction and purpose.

The MBTI is the most used and well known psychometric instrument in the world. I have taught its background, run assessments, and coached it developmentally in 26 countries, so far. And fortunately, it is culturally sensitized to be able to do so in most.

Psychological Underpinnings

A bit of background. The founding psychoanalytical great-grandfather of the MBTI is Carl Jung, but he didn't develop it, only that his theories helped inform Isabel Myers and Katharine Briggs later in the century. No doubt you will have heard of him. Jung, Sigmund Freud, and Alfred Adler in the early 20th century were peers with very differing perspectives on psychological development. Ultimately Freud became known for his theory of psychoanalysis, Adler individual psychology, and Jung analytical psychology. There is a possible Jung uncredited quote that "if you don't know yourself well, the world will tell you" at the start of the chapter, but I like it anyway. As with all theorists their ontological view of how the world works really governs each's ideas. For example, Freud was interested in the external and internal forces that drive behavior, but he was trained as a neurologist and unsurprisingly his focus was primarily brain function. Adler believed that we could shape our own lives. He wasn't oblivious to social forces but his training as a medical doctor was more on the body as a whole and the feelings we have. Perhaps most will know him for the use of the words introduced earlier about the conditions of 'inferiority and superiority complex.' Freud was critical of introversion being an orientation to the world that is more negative than the extroverted world. Freud and Adler in particular had perspectives which sat at completely opposite ends of the spectrum particularly around introversion and extroversion. So why does this matter? Well, Jung took a more dynamic and fluid view. He regarded the introversion and extroversion orientation as more of a continuum where we are able to move sometimes towards one or another depending on many other factors. But he also explained something which underpins the MBTI: that we all have a leaning towards certain preferred ways of being. In 1921 he published *Psychological Types*, where he proposes we can group people according to a psychological type. He describes how we have two mental functions: perceiving — taking in information, and judging — the process of organizing that information and how we use it to make decisions. We all use both functions but with a preference leaning towards one or another reflecting our dominant preference. He also explained his thinking around the continuum of high introverts to high extroverts which are referred to as attitudes or orientations, and describe how we relate to the outer world. He describes the juxtaposition of introverts from extroverts as differences in how we prefer to use energy and recover energy from the world around us and from inside ourselves. The movement of energy provides a very important part of the model of gravitas and how we can use our energy as a means to influence both our thinking and the behavior of others. Gravitas is as much a quality of the interaction with others and our perspective on how we see the world and where we fit in, as it is an inner mental processing function illuminating our feelings and decision-making. In addition, Jung's idea that we have preferences of how we behave that constantly move along a continuum is another critical concept, because when we learn to adapt to different situations it offers a degree of control over our effectiveness and that of others through the temperament modification. Let me briefly explain what is meant by preferences of the mental functions and attitudes and orientations. The MBTI functions and orientations image shows the 4 key preference pairs from what is called the Step I report.

Extraversion: You focus on the outside world and get energy through interacting with people and/or doing things.	Introversion: You focus on the inner world and get energy though reflecting on information, ideas and/or concepts.
Sensing: You notice and trust facts, details and present realities.	Intuition: You attend to and trust interrelationships, theories and future possibilities.
Thinking: You make decisions using logical analysis to achieve objectivity.	Feeling: You make decisions using person-centered values to achieve harmony.
Judging: You tend to be organized and orderly and to make decisions quickly.	Perceiving: You tend to be flexible and adaptable and to keep your options open as long as possible.

Table 6.1: MBTI Functions and Orientations

If you want more detailed explanations of each of the dimensions any search on the Internet or AI can provide sufficient information. However, there are a few myths that I would like to dispel:

- Extraversion is the same as extroverted, and intraversion is the same as introverted: Not necessarily but mostly and perhaps that is my interpretation at play. There are quiet people with a preference for extraversion and there are expressive or gregarious by nature introverts. That is where the MBTI Step II report has more depth, which is what introversion preferred people really want to know!
- If you have a preference for feeling it does not mean you are emotional. Not necessarily at least. In fact, I have a preference for feeling but three out of my five facets lean towards thinking.

- Perceiving means perceptive and judging means judgmental. Wrong — in every way.

In the figure below, I have shown my MBTI 'type,' and you will see that the report shows the degree of preference I have each of the four key elements.

One of the first things you learn about teaching or coaching with the MBTI is to find a way to bring it to life for those who have never heard of it. The one I recall most vividly is being asked to sign your name with your preferred writing hand and then switching to the other. In most cases people can immediately describe why the second signature felt awkward, less practiced, and not natural, but also that they could do it and improve with practice. Jung had suggested that if children's development was pushed outside of their natural mode it might create illness. We know now that in the earlier part of the 20th century children were sometimes forced to write with their right hand, and in some cases had their left hand tied behind them. It seems pretty extreme now but as a left hander myself I was always interested that this was done during my parents' lifetime rather than some barbaric medieval period, and later we learned that some would grow up with learning difficulties most likely attributed by not being able to use their preferred side. The importance of finding a comfortable fit with your level of self-awareness allied to your 'type' is to reflect on whether you are

INFP	VERY CLEAR	CLEAR	MODERATE	SLIGHT	MODERATE	CLEAR	VERY CLEAR	
EXTRAVERSION E				→				INTROVERSION I
SENSING S					——→			INTUITION N
THINKING T				→				FEELING F
JUDGING J					——→			PERCEIVING P

RESULTS INTROVERSION 1 INTUITION 14 FEELING 2 PERCEIVING 20

Figure 6.2: MBTI Clarity of Preferences

having to work outside of your preferences, and therefore possibly damaging your mental state and your potential to build gravitas. This is especially important on the introversion and extraversion scale because those with a preference for introversion will need more time and mental space to recover energy and learn to relate to others more consciously.

The MBTI is also not a psychological test. There isn't a pass or fail or an ideal score. Strictly speaking it is not a pure personality assessment. But I think that makes it ideal as a first step to build self-awareness. There are two levels of the report: Step I and Step II. The first creates a report showing which preferred psychological type you might be out of 16 options. Understandably some people don't like that. Sixteen isn't really a sufficient enough group of types to cover everyone. Isn't it? Well, no one wants to be put in a box but actually it is more complex. The first level only begins to group broad sets of behaviors into categories of similar preferences into what are called types. It doesn't mean anyone in the same box with any others is exactly the same. It simply describes a general leaning towards our general orientation to how we live. In that sense it is only four times better than the DISC report. However, the Step II report addresses the variances in each type providing a further 40 facets of the 16 types. If you have access to it, use it, but you will normally need to work with a qualified practitioner to understand the second step properly. Unless you already are one of course, and you will therefore have moved on by now! I believe Step I is sufficient, for now.

In order to demonstrate how useful Step II is I can offer an example. I have fewer facet preferences for feeling over thinking but remain an INFP. Despite having an introverted preference one can see I also have a very strong preference for expressiveness.

I hope this might be helpful for you to help appreciate that you can be introverted, as I am, but also expressive, which in

20 FACETS FROM THE STEP II™ ASSESSMENT
MIDZONE

E							
	Initiating			◆		Receiving	I
	Expressive	←―――				Contained	
	Gregarious				――→	Intimate	
	Active				――→	Reflective	
	Enthusiastic				――→	Quiet	
S	Concrete			――→		Abstract	**N**
	Realistic				――→	Imaginative	
	Practical			――→		Conceptual	
	Experiential				――→	Theoretical	
	Traditional				――→	Original	
T	Logical				――→	Empathetic	**F**
	Reasonable	←―――				Compassionate	
	Questioning				―――→	Accommodating	
	Critical	←―――				Accepting	
	Tough	←―――				Tender	
J	Systematic			―――→		Casual	**P**
	Planful				―――→	Open-Ended	
	Early Starting				――→	Pressure-Prompted	
	Scheduled				―――→	Spontaneous	
	Methodical	←―――				Emergent	

Figure 6.3: The MBTI Step II Report Summary

the case of many that have met me can make me seem like I am more extroverted in character when interacting with others.

If you already have a previous report or decided to complete an assessment as a result of reading thus far you will have worked out if you think you 'fit' with what the report says. The 'fit' is rather like trying a pair of shoes on. Do they feel right? What do you like or not like? It can take time to find a true fit and that is not surprising because it is based on your input solely. That's where the benefit of a 360-degree analysis can come into play. However, you can share your report with others you trust to get a more complete perspective.

Chapter Seven

Gravitas through a Personal Conceptual Encounter

Building on the model of gravitas presented earlier, let's now get an understanding of your gravitas state and assess your strengths. I suggest you journal your responses, but use whatever medium you are most comfortable with and address the questions below. This is the first conceptual encounter and is a private reflective practice:

1. What do you understand by the term 'gravitas'? Use your own words.
   a. Which words or sentences did you record that relate to the 5 constructs of gravitas?
   b. Were there any words that you used that were markedly different?
   c. Would you therefore replace any of the main construct titles or swap any around?
2. How do you know when someone has gravitas?
3. Think of people you've encountered who you consider having gravitas. Describe them.
4. What is the effect these people seem to have on others and you?
5. Do you have any gravitas role models? — If so, who are they and what do they have that appeals to you?
6. When is gravitas most important to you?
7. Describe a time or a situation when you felt your gravitas was missing.
   a. What about your gravitas was missing?
   b. Relate these to any of the 21 temperaments in your own language.

8. What are some of the barriers that might stop you improving your gravitas?
   a. What sort of thoughts might hold you back from developing gravitas?
   b. What behaviors might hold you back from developing gravitas?
   c. How have you attempted to overcome these before?

Guidance on completing the answers:

- Record a proper narrative of your ideas rather than just one-word answers.
- Focus on providing specific examples and write them out as paragraphs.
- Look for patterns of your experiences.
- If you can record your answers on an electronic device try to have someone else ask the questions.
- Listen to the words you use and compare them to my description of gravitas.
- Where are they similar or different?
- Why do you think that is?

If you find that getting into the detail of your answers first too difficult draw a spider diagram. The key steps to creating a spider diagram if you have not done so before are:

- Step one is to draw a shape at the center which you might call Gravitas and Me.
- Record your answer to the first question by drawing a line out of the center shape and write or draw your initial thoughts.
- Don't make the words you use too long. You will use this as a basis to provide a more detailed narrative later.

- Gradually branch out from the line to add more ideas.
- When you move to the next question start a new line.
- If you can, add colors to make the diagram more memorable and interesting.

You will need to add more detail in written form or do a separate diagram for each question. The next action is to highlight common themes. Use a highlighter pen if you have written your answers. If you have typed them out, you could use a highlighter function, or you may use the method I used which is to record my answers and then transcribe them using software. This method is more likely to result in longer answers but you end up with more of your own data. The idea is to create an elegant and parsimonious description of gravitas as it is experienced by you. Why do this and not simply use my models? Well, as I have explained in the book so far, I found gravitas moves around and we need to know how you fit into it or may even adapt it. Certainly, every situation presents a different pressure on your gravitas. If there were just ten golden rules or tips to gravitas (for example), everyone would be able to turn it on or switch it off at will. However, it is not like that. As essential as it is, it can also be elusive. Therefore, the title of the book, *Where Did My Gravitas Go?* As you become used to being living learners with the use of some of my techniques, I believe you should keep coming back to your conceptions, test and refine them, and eventually build your own approaches. As I will describe in the next chapter on coaching yourself, there is a cycle of reflective practice that is constant. There isn't one way to hit a tennis ball, golf ball, or football, is there? There is some solid groundwork that can work for most people but then we refine this according to our strengths, weaknesses, the climate, situation, and of course our opponent. Gravitas pressures are the same.

Gravitas Assessment: Your Tree of Life

Until you make the unconscious conscious, it will direct your life and you will call it fate.

— Carl Jung

The third part of your gravitas personal assessment aims to uncover your values and motivations as a leader. Although self-reflection can feel a little unproductive for some people, I have found it to be one of the most valued aspects when leading groups away from the workplace. It's as if there isn't enough time to do so when performing under the microscope at work, but our alignment of those aspects we see as important and how we behave and what we choose to do as a profession provides a useful mirror. When the alignment is not congruent it lacks the sincerity we need in leaders. The impact of exercises of this type can have a profound impact on decisions we take next in life and how we relate to others.

The process is known as psychodynamics or psychodynamic psychology. The aim is to make connections between our unconscious and conscious states to help understand our personality, behaviors, motivations and values. Carl Jung referenced the importance of making the unconscious conscious to become more complete, and had justified this by suggesting that if you don't you may end up seeing your future life as just fate rather than decisions you have chosen to make. Here is how the process works.

The exercise was developed in partnership with my research participants and is called 'the tree of life,' and I must emphasize that this is not connected to the similarly titled exercise used in some schools, sometimes controversially, that seeks to understand someone's family history. A lot of our values and motivations are rooted in our early life and as such the tree is represented as a drawing of our life beginning with the roots of the tree that then becomes strong through the trunk of the tree before branching out in many different directions. The branches will have many leaves on it, but instead of an actual leaf I would like you to envisage buildings, people, events, and so on. Some branches will be strong, some will wither or even die. Some roots will be thicker and longer than others, and as they form into a trunk, knots will develop. These represent decisive milestones, some negative, some positive, but are important to you.

Try to reflect on people that have influenced your life in either a good or bad way. It may even be one encounter that has left a mark on you. Note key places you have lived, and places you have been to and worked in. Remember buildings, forms of transport, moments of joy and sadness. It's your life of course!

Let's go through the instructions.

- Find a quiet time and space where you won't be interrupted.
- Use a large piece of blank paper (at least A3, or 11x17 inches) and colored pens.
- Check in with yourself to make sure you feel centered — even breathing, no pains, and imagine yourself somewhere beautiful and have all the time in the world.
- I always suggest that you draw the tree on a portrait-orientated sheet of paper, but really just find some way of comfortably representing your tree.
- Cast your mind back over your life and initially just list aspects, people, events, successes, failures, activities, passions, and places through your life from birth to today.
- Consider where your tree will be — in a wood, a forest, a mountain, by a river, even alone in a desert, and sketch that out. Also, what is the sky like? Is it moody, grey, sunny, and how is the weather — windy, rain, snowing, still?
- Once you have represented your ground and sky, start drawing your roots. Use colors, images, and words to describe why each root is important.

- As you get to the base of the trunk — reflect on the rings of the trunk. Each ring could represent a year in your life or as much as a decade or significant age. You may want to draw the tree rings alongside your tree drawing to create a 3-dimensional view. For many I have found that reflecting on each year or significant period of your life helps to surface the key changes in your life.
- The most important events in your early life to young adulthood (zero to 25 years old) should be captured in your image of the trunk, and signified as tree knots.
- As you branch out from your trunk draw as many as you feel reflect the next stages of your life. Get creative with what the branches represent and what is hanging from each branch. Now is the time to bring in a little artistry with images and colors.
- As the tree grows towards your current state begin to reflect what might happen next if you make decisions that align to your values.
- Which moments on your tree are most significant?
- Which people are most significant?
- Try to list your values that have developed in your life and how these relate to your roots and your trunk. (An example of personal values is shown in the figure below, but there are many more of course.)
- Which aspects of your tree contribute positively or negatively to your own gravitas?
- Looking ahead — what key choices do you anticipate, where do you envision your life in five years, and what would you like to change?
- Finally reflect on how you would tell your story through the tree to another person, and practice telling it. Try to limit your story to five minutes. It's very difficult to do!

Accountability	Faith	Positive attitude
Accuracy	Family	Power
Adventure	Freedom	Progress
Beauty	Friendship	Prosperity, Wealth
Calm	Goodness	Punctuality
Challenge	Gratitude	Quality
Change	Hard work	Respect for others
Collaboration	Harmony	Safety
Commitment	Honesty	Security
Communication	Honor	Simplicity
Community	Independence	Skill
Continuous improvement	Integrity	Speed
	Justice	Stability
Cooperation	Knowledge	Strength
Coordination	Leadership	Success
Creativity	Love	Teamwork
Decisiveness	Loyalty	Timeliness
Discipline	Openness	Tradition
Discovery	Peace, Non-violence	Tranquility
Efficiency	Perfection	Trust
Excellence	Personal Growth	Truth
Fairness	Pleasure	Wisdom

Table 7.1: Examples of Personal Values

Over the years I have led this exercise I have seen some of the most elaborate and odd interpretations of a tree. Some almost are pieces of art in their own right and could hang on a wall, and some might have been drawn with a straight edge and a few dots like a cross between a radar or an electrocardiograph machine. I recommend the creative approach even if your drawing skills are not something you are proud of. In the classroom sometimes, people are unsure about revealing their emotionally challenging periods and choose not to record them. Primarily it is because in a group setting the exercise requires you to tell your story to another person or more, and for the listener to say what they have heard and help the person sharing their story to understand what values or what matters to them most and how that may influence behaviors. Sometimes, however, it is not just the sharing rather it is unearthing an incredibly difficult situation or time that is simply too painful to bring up, even privately.

If you have someone you can share your story with it will add to the reflective process, but if you wish to be private that is perfectly fine. If you opt for the former approach, it is likely you will be sharing your life story with someone you know. That may make it more comfortable for you, but it does mean the listener already has some preformed opinions on your values and behaviors, and what you find difficult. The listener writes down what they hear and the values they think matter to you. (See list below.) If you choose the private route the only difference will be the reflections on what the listener hears. Whichever route chosen, record your life story, and if you have the technology at your disposal use a transcription piece of software that you might have on a tablet, phone or laptop for example. It won't record all of your words perfectly, but you should be able to get a reasonably good record of the words and situations you have used. Listen to your story and write down what values you hear, and look at the transcript and highlight words you use that are interesting and help to describe you as you think you are to yourself and others.

1. Next try to distil your list of values to a number between five to ten.
2. Write out what the value looks like in your life as an outcome.
3. Then write down three behaviors that you exhibit that reflect each value.
4. Are there any gaps between your behaviors and the value you see as important? For example, if health was

an important value as an aim in life but your behavior reflected not exercising or eating well, it would be easy to see the discrepancy and what to address. Or perhaps autonomy is a value outcome you aim for, but you work in a micromanaged role at work.
5. How will you address these gaps?
6. Do these values motivate you or are there other motivators that aren't reflected in the values?

When you have completed your masterpiece and the reflection exercises, we move on to where we need to work on improving our gravitas. At this stage you are simply making notes on general thoughts you have to help you focus on the subsequent stages of the assessment where you will need to recall more detail. Consider your responses to the following questions.

1. What are real situations where you needed your gravitas but it was missing?
2. How would having gravitas have changed those situations for the better?
3. What are your fears?
4. What don't you like about yourself?
5. On the flip side what do you like about yourself?
6. Where are you most assured and confident?
7. When do you feel most like yourself — who are you with and what situations?
8. Where have you found your gravitas strengths?

Gravitas Assessment: Temperament
Scoring and Constructs

The next reflective exercise is to gauge where you assess your gravitas performance on each of the five constructs and 21 temperaments.

In order to make your assessment as accurate as possible try to recall a specific situation at work that was important to you. You can complete the exercise for as many situations as you wish including those where you felt your gravitas was lacking and those where you felt you had it!

Under each construct write a corresponding number down that reflects where you are on the gravitas scale. Unlike many scales this runs from 1 to 6 and reflects when you have too little or too much of something.

The scale works like this:

Number 1 = Too Low/little
Number 2 = Low/little
Number 3 = Moderate
Number 4 = Sufficient
Number 5 = High
Number 6 = Too High/much

When you have scored every temperament add them together, so you have a score for each construct. And finally add the construct scores together for a combined gravitas score.

Begin with a paragraph describing the specific situation and then record in your journal or something similar your responses:

Courage	Score
Demonstrate decisiveness without arrogance	
Be assertive with empathy	
Be authentic with integrity	
Take risks with enthusiasm	
Find strength to face negativity and failure	
Total	

Confidence	Score
Unflustered and composed under pressure	
Manage and be accepting of uncertainty	
Be comfortable in one's own skin with an identity	
Have purpose and be purposeful	
Total	

Credibility	Score
Actions and words have congruence	
Maintain dignity and poise	
Have imagination and be informed	
Have humility and openness	
Total	

Control	Score
Find and recover balance	
Be prepared	
Build climate	
Change the mood of oneself and others	
Total	

Communication	Score
Be direct and precise	
Know when to communicate and when not to	
Maintain clarity of thought	
Adapt and translate to build understanding	
Total	

Total Gravitas Score:

What do the scores mean? Firstly, there will be crossovers in areas and there should be because that is how patterns emerge. Are there any patterns across different situations? The overall

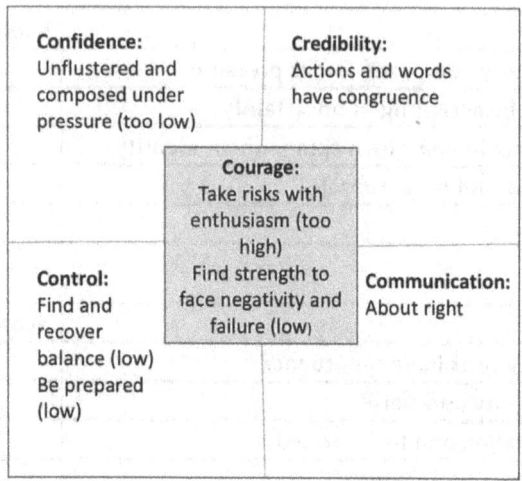

Figure 7.1: Temperament Development Examples

score for a construct is as important as looking at the extremes on the scale but even so if a construct is over 20 it will highlight an area that you may be overdoing and might consider requires development. Individual temperament scores that are one and two also indicate an area for development. As I have gathered data with the questions I often find people have between five to eight areas they want to concentrate on, which feels much more manageable than 21! For example, putting my own cards on the table my development areas were:

Gravitas Assessment: Goals and Role Models

The last of the reflective exercises is to answer five overall questions for each of the constructs as shown in the above figure, and as we compile your overall development goals, to answer five further questions. Write your answers down in a journal or on another platform for the first five questions:

1. Courage: How are you resilient?
2. Confidence: What gives you self-esteem?

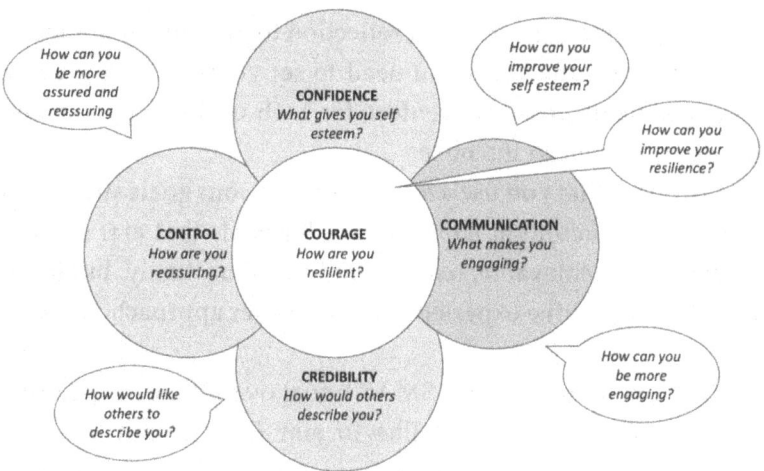

Figure 7.2: Construct Development Questions

3. Credibility: How would others describe you?
4. Control: How are you reassuring?
5. Communication: What makes you engaging?

Now that you have completed the reflection exercises, we need to combine the activities, to set some goals and mental images to work with, and inspire you to act in the future. You should have in your journal or recorded elsewhere:

1. Your MBTI preferences on the four scales (and possibly the 20 facets from Step II). You may have chosen another personality instrument, and if you are comfortable with it — use it.
2. Your gravitas answers and thoughts from your personal conceptual encounter questions.
3. Your key values and motivators from the tree of your life.
4. A list of the key temperaments on which you need to focus your development.
5. Your five conceptual encounter answers to the initial questions in this chapter.

This last exercise moves from reflection to planning and focuses exclusively on the goals you need to set yourself, and gravitas role models or possibly mentors for each of the temperaments for development in the boxes.

I propose that you use a structure to set your goals such as the SMART goal acronym which stands for goals that are: specific, measurable, achievable, realistic and timed or timely, but if you have had a positive experience with another approach, use that.

1. Now write out your SMART goal overall for the personal gravitas you would like to aim for. Explain how this reflects your strengths from your reflective exercises, and where these challenge your less preferred or less developed areas. Add why this is important to you from the perspective of where you wish your tree to grow, and how to live up to your values.
2. Next, record your five answers for each of the five overall constructs as shown in the above figure:
    i. How can you improve your resilience?
    ii. How can you instill confidence in others?
    iii. How would you like others to describe you?
    iv. How can you be more assured and reassuring?
    v. How can you be more engaging?

Finally, you are going to do two things; First, to write out a goal for each of the temperaments you wish to develop. Be very specific and explain what types of situations you will need to develop them in. For example, choose approximately five:

Temperament and Situations 1:
Temperament and Situations 2:
Temperament and Situations 3:
Temperament and Situations 4:
Temperament and Situations 5:

And now to complete the development goal process identify a series of images of role models and/or mentors for your overall gravitas and each of the temperaments you wish to focus on. As you will see in the next section on your inner coach, the importance of having a visual image is essential for the effectiveness of coaching yourself. If you happen to know someone who is your role model you may prefer to think of them as a mentor but in all other cases they remain a role model or even an avatar to hold in your mind.

Answer the following questions:

Who is your overall gravitas goal role model or mentor?
1. Within the construct of courage — who do you imagine or know is a role model for you and for which temperament or temperaments?
2. Within the construct of confidence — who do you imagine or know is a role model for you and for which temperament or temperaments?
3. Within the construct of credibility — who do you imagine or know is a role model for you and for which temperament or temperaments?
4. Within the construct of control — who do you imagine or know is a role model for you and for which temperament or temperaments?
5. Within the construct of communication — who do you imagine or know is a role model for you and for which temperament or temperaments?

If you built your development goals from the exercises on a digital platform, add a screen shot of the image of the person or people from your last exercise to reinforce memory recall as we now move into the development of your inner coach and the value of somatic and image based coaching as a tool for self-growth.

Part Three
Performing

Chapter Eight

Meet Your Inner Gravitas Coaching Team – *Performance Coach, Psychotherapist Coach, and Public Relations Coach*

Nearly all of us have a little voice inside our head. For some it's a noise that rarely goes away but for those that think that it's surely something everyone has you might be surprised to know that some people have never experienced it at all. Surprised? Well to be clear we all have thoughts and feelings, but some people don't have that additional narrative that follows. If you are one of the few that doesn't, this chapter might be challenging to say the least!

A part of self-talk, as it is often referred to, can often be the inner voice of doubt, worry, and negativity. If our empathy works well we will tend to keep those thoughts to ourselves for fear of the effect it may have on the judgement of others. We might talk to ourselves out loud to do anything such as self-motivate, lift our spirits, test out our thinking, and indeed sometimes chastise ourselves for something we have done. It's certainly not exclusively inward negativity and outward positivity but it is when we are in the company of others that we are more likely to internalize self-talk, and when we are alone feel safe to speak out loud. It is all self-talk. I will explain how to support a lack of self-talk later in this section, but for the majority of those reading I want to explain how we can use our own minds to enable us to coach ourselves to take gravitas actions.

Many of us will have heard athletes outwardly shouting about their game or event mid-performance for everyone to hear, and it is often that mix of berating themselves and telling themselves what to do. Most recently as I type the draft of this section I watched Nick Kyrgios in the 2022 Wimbledon final against Novak Djokovic ranting, shouting in fact, at himself about how many chances he needed, over and over again. Entertaining for some, annoying for others, but for Nick it seemed to be both a performance admonishment and motivational talk. I also recall that rather than shouting, Andy Murray the former world number one referred to a coaching 'to-do' list he had underneath his chair to remind himself of what to do and how to think during his match against Gilles Simon at the ATP500 tournament in Rotterdam, and again at the Australian Open in 2015, and talking to himself a little more quietly. We can lip read the pictures of others often in team sports where the microphone cannot get close enough to pick up their words. But there also others who seem to say very little, whose expressions do not alter that much. You can be sure their minds are whirring around and talk to themselves just as much, however. What we are unlikely to see or hear is the surgeon, mid-surgery, talking out loud to themselves (I might be wrong about that!), the judge mid-court proceedings or the actor on stage expressing out loud inner thoughts, unless that was the intention. Nevertheless, you can guarantee that the voice inside their head is live, listening and talking. It would not be very confidence inspiring, appropriate, and indeed be very confusing if they started to let their inner voice speak out. Even as I write this section I am talking to myself about my back aching and that I must get out and walk around and self-manage regularly. So, you get the picture. Or at least most of you will. So how do we self-coach rather than just self-talk? I'll begin with the subject of coaching itself as this is how I have introduced and worked with my clients on building their gravitas either one to one or in teams or groups with the aim that they will eventually be able to go away and self-coach, practice, reflect, and adapt.

The Role of Coaching

As a distinct form of personal development, coaching has received a lot of attention over the past 30 years, spurred on especially from John Whitmore's (1992) book introducing his GROW model and the role of coaching to help unlock the maximum potential of an individual. Of course, coaching in specific contexts such as sports or the arts has been at the forefront of skills and performance development for many centuries. It could be argued that coaching might be thousands of years old. The ancient Greek philosopher and storyteller Socrates' form of questioning is one of the foundations of modern coaching approaches, but it is unlikely that anyone described it in that way at that time. Socratic questioning has been linked to the processes of logic, reason, and law for many years, and indeed Greek philosophers were often described as the original teachers in society. Walk around any teaching hospital and you will hear group-based Socratic questioning at work. In the hospital environment the teaching doctor ask a series of questions to individual doctors in training, one by one around the group, gradually deducing or reducing a patient's particular symptoms down to a thorough diagnosis. For example a week ago I was in a neuro-ophthalmology appointment, which I have every six months due to my eye disease, and in walked my usual specialist with two other junior level doctors at different levels of their specialist training. I asked my usual doctor about the use of a new type of eyedrop to support my existing one. Rather than answering she asked the other two in turn for their thoughts. She knew the answer but she started with the most junior and then asked for confirmation or alternative views from the next one in line until confirming herself. In some way our self-talk coaching reflects this Socratic process. We might begin with our frustration about how we handled a relationship with someone in the past. On reflection we realize we might have handled it differently but ask why we didn't in that moment.

When presented to a new encounter our Socratic inner coaching begins. "Remember this situation before," it says. And we reply, "Yes of course." "Well what did we learn?" And so, we try to coach ourselves into handling it better this time. However, this time in the context of gravitas I want to give you the tools to help you coach yourself more effectively. As I wrote in the previous chapter, in the sports arena, self-coaching, and on field, track or on court coaching might take place but it's the combination of the psychology of coaching and our physical embodiment that matters and makes the psychology complex.

Your Two Selfs

Tim Gallwey's *The Inner Game of Tennis* (1975) was and is a fascinating book with an insight into how our minds (intentionally plural) play tricks with us. Master the mind and the performance will accelerate but the real skill is the visualizing and doing. Let me explain. He suggested we have two types of mind or self. Type one and type two. In a game of tennis, we might observe two games being played. The outer game we physically observe and experience, and an inner one in the mind. In professional sports, for those with an interest in them, you'll have heard many times that the mental side becomes ever more important. After all, the talented sports person can perform a skill, a shot, a move, many times to the highest level but not every time, not against every opponent, in different climates with different people watching. That's part of the frustration. Outside of the sports world we might think about how we get along with others. It is pretty inconsistent, not everyone likes us or us them. Some people somehow bring out the worst in us. It's so frustrating and it plays on the mind. The more frustrated the mind gets the more impossible it seems to stop thinking about whatever it is that is stopping us from being at our best. What we are aiming to achieve is a calm state of mind, a state of being. We'll get into this in more detail in a bit but let's take a look at coaching through some different lenses before we turn back to coaching ourselves.

It's useful to begin with an understanding of what exactly you are coaching. Are you looking simply to improve your idea of performance? Do you have a problem from a personality perspective? Are you trying to coach your gravitas in a specific context such as at work or leading others, or just socially for example? Are you looking for a more holistic improvement of yourself without context or goals? Does any of that matter? Yes, it does.

When you conducted your own assessment of your perceptions of gravitas and where you fit with the model proposed here, you reflected on what it is about you that makes you who you are. Many of these thoughts will have noticed both strengths and weaknesses. And some of these strengths become weaknesses when you overdo them. So, is there anything you might call dysfunctional about you? Your internal psychotherapy coach needs to know but we are often blind to our own dysfunctions. One person I coached recognized that every few years he would self-sabotage his career. He didn't know why but over time started to wonder if he saw himself as a fraud and didn't deserve success at work — his version of the previously described imposter syndrome. He worried others would see through him, so before they did he would abandon his colleagues and role and restart somewhere else. So, he came to me wanting to build gravitas with others and help understand where his self-doubt came from. In effect, we had two stories running but we couldn't work on one without recognizing the other. The second point is understanding the power of social and organizational structures around you. "No man is an island," wrote John Donne comparing people to countries. Our reflections begin with ourselves but what impact do culture and cultures have on allowing you to be the real you?

Let's imagine ourselves as gravitas athletes for a moment. We have a coach that is always thinking about the macro us. Where are we heading, what do we want out of life and who else out there impacts us. That voice is talking to our inner coach thinking about who we are and what makes us special and not so special. Our unique qualities are our strengths if we can learn how to use them. These two are talking to our outward coaches. They consider what we do and how well we do it. Others measure and will judge us on these areas, and in turn that feeds how we feel about ourselves and so on. They represent a kind of public relations team and a performance team. But there are more coaches in our team. We haven't even considered yet our physical side. We don't simply show up as giant brains on legs. The body as you know already tells us a lot about how we are feeling and transmits energy to others. It might also appear to suck the life out of others at times, but our inner coach needs to pay attention to it.

In the coaching psychology world this hasn't gone unnoticed. A few alternative approaches have emerged with very specific links to embodiment. Sieler (2010) and Matthews (2013) proposed this more holistic approach to coaching incorporating the mind and the body, which might be described as a type of 'ontological coaching.'

"The essential goal of the coach is to be a catalyst for change by respectfully and constructively triggering a shift in the coachee's way of being to enable him or her to develop perceptions and behaviors that were previously unavailable."

Our gravitas personal assessment included the use of an analysis of language through the conceptual encounter self-interview to help us understand ourselves. Our coaching team is also listening for what is hidden; however, not in our verbal language but in moods, emotions, and the body. This somatic reaction is reflected as embodied connections between the mind and body. In order to work with ourselves to help explore our embodied reactions, our inner coach needs to develop a kinesthetic awareness of our own body responses (Ratener, 2014) before being sufficiently skilled to work with our gravitas. Beyond kinesthetic awareness our gravitas athlete needs to look after our body too. Our somatic and mind responses can easily become negative if we haven't paid attention to our health, nutrition, and musculoskeletal architecture. If we find ourselves overreacting to someone who is a challenge to our gravitas, but we are tired from overindulgence on a late night or stressed from sleepless nights, it will be unsurprising if we suffer inner anxiety and outward inappropriate responses. It's going to happen to some so we will have to be aware of these triggers, and also somewhat forgiving to ourselves.

For us our inner coach needs a type of coaching andragogy, which act as a set of beliefs that we mentally sign up to. What do I mean by that?

Your Three Principles of Coaching Andragogy

1. Human Experience: My actual experiences are at the heart of developing inner and outer gravitas.
2. Self-knowing: I cannot develop gravitas without knowing myself. This is a cyclic process of reflection, practice, adaptation, and reflection.
3. Learning from Play: I encourage myself to experiment with new ideas. Consciously introduce physical activity, and have an equal balance of cognitive processing.

Let's just remind ourselves what coaching is fundamentally about. Learning. Coaching yourself isn't easy. It's hard to be objective with yourself and coaching will often take place under pressure. Therefore practice, observation, and self-reflection are essential. There is some solid groundwork already conducted on how we as adults learn, and it is important for us to recognize this to ensure we are patient and forgiving with ourselves. Learning patterns do change as we progress from children to young adults, midlife adults, and then older. And whilst our affirming experiences evolve so do our resistances and fears. So, let's dig a little into the adult learning process.

Remember the idea presented earlier that we have two types of self, referred to as type one and type two? Good. When we learn to do something there are likely to be a series of instructions on what we are supposed to do. For example, learning to drive a car. Most of us will have done this, and will recall how we get ourselves into a safe and comfortable driving position: can we reach the pedals, can we rest both hands on the wheel and be able to turn it full circle whilst keeping contact with the wheel? Can we see out of the mirrors? Adjust all as needed and belt up. And so, it goes on. Mind you, in my teens my 1970s Alfa Romeo made all these things a near impossibility but at least I was flexible then! Anyway, at this phase of learning we are consciously remembering the process before we start to put things into practice. I'll assume here that you are familiar with the learning steps linking the mind with actions from being unconsciously incompetent, consciously incompetent, consciously competent, to unconsciously competent. The competent word doesn't really sound friendly, but you have the idea that first we don't know what we don't know, then we learn something but are not too good at it, and eventually we can do it without really thinking. In reality you are of course conscious, and even experienced skilled drivers have to sometimes reconcentrate on the basics because of perhaps appalling weather or driving when fatigued, on the other side of road, or with an unfamiliar vehicle, and so on. I recently sat with a driver who described themselves as experienced, but they had never driven a manual (stick shift) car and thought it was easy. In fact, they described it to me as, "it's about the same as an auto, but you have to press the left pedal more, then release the pedal and go." Can you imagine how the reality hit him? Yep, you're right. It was way more difficult than the steps sounded. Once the pressure of other drivers, lights, roundabouts (traffic circles), and the other driving duties were combined we kangarooed at an alarming pace into an embarrassing stall. If I had been drinking a cup of coffee 'en route' I would have been drenched and slightly warm. As he thought through the process he was simply unable to somatically match it with smooth movement. When I learnt to ski in my thirties I recall exactly the same frustration as I hurtled towards a train of small children on the nursery slopes. I knew what I was supposed to do from the lessons I'd taken but my body would not do it. I became increasingly rigid together with an ever more terrified state of mind. Moving back to the driving metaphor again, I used to be an executive in the automotive world and even headed a world-renowned chauffeur driving school as part of my remit. There are many tasks for a chauffeur but a primary one is not to have your passenger drenched in the drink they are consuming on their journey. Learning to drive smoothly, and quickly when necessary, and safely is a new learning process for a skill that most think they have already accomplished. As mature adults the instructions associated with driving smoothly are more difficult to remember and put in place. The school needed other learning stimulants rather than instructions to help teach its chauffeurs. We borrowed one from the three-time Formula One world champion, Sir Jackie Stewart, who in his Principles of Performance Driving courses with Ford many years ago had a novel approach. On the hood or bonnet was stuck a giant rubber bowl. About the circumference of a very large paella dish and as deep as a satellite dish. In the bowl he placed a tennis ball. As the driver drove around the track their aim was to keep the ball inside of the bowl whilst driving as fast as possible. It focuses the mind perfectly. Instead of 50 things to think about you have one that is visual and kinesthetic. I had the opposite learning experience years before this with another automotive company when those of us with corporate cars were required to do the UK's Advanced Driving Certificate. I had been driving for nearly 20 years at that point and was doing OK. However, with a new instructor aboard we headed into the busy streets of London where concentration is always necessary but now I was furnished with endless new instructions and directions. My little brain was hard at work trying to put everything into practice. There was no time for my inner performance coach to get a look in. The brain coach was way too busy. In addition, my body coach was reminding me that I'm too tense, asking what I'm doing with my hands, why my teeth are clenched, and my jaw is wired shut. It's hard to do in the moment.

Well heading back to the innovative coaching approach developed by Tim Gallwey: he found the same type of challenges that I have described learning to drive or ski, when teaching people to play tennis. Learning to master a tennis stroke or shot was traditionally a process of learning the instructions of grip, positioning, eye focus, swing, and follow through. Easy when you know how to and easy to remember the steps but for a beginner very hard to execute. He recognized that we have an inner game taking place whilst we learn, where we lose concentration, get nervous, and doubt ourselves. And if it doesn't work we start to castigate ourselves. The mind develops a series of habits and those become serious barriers to overcome. If you have found yourselves reading this because you want to develop your gravitas, anyway why else would you, then you probably have some bad mental habits and human experiences you want to learn to overcome and charge your path forward to perform better. Going back to the tennis beginner, Gallwey suggested that the learning should begin with focusing on the unconscious mind not the conscious one. Quite different from the learning process I described earlier. Imagine trying to teach a one-year-old how to walk. They copy, they observe, they practice, they fall down, get up, and try again. The tennis player in this process is about to do the same. It's a natural calmer way of learning and that's where both the two types of 'self' come in to play.

> Self 1 – is the brain which is often fueled with negativity, doubt, and anxiety
> Self 2 – is the body which is the more intuitive self and does the doing

The natural pedagogic process moves from Self 1 to Self 2 and back to 1 again. Gallwey's tennis coachee wasn't given instructions, he was asked to watch him hit ten crosscourt forehands. The only real instruction was to ask his coachee to copy him. Instead of trying to remember, the player simply copies with additional comments such as try to hit it in that direction or towards a certain point on the court. The real goal is getting the brain's two Selfs talk to link up with the body seamlessly to achieve a state of what has been called flow.

Our inner coaching team needs to switch modes to one of positivity and more confidence where it is the intuitive doing Self 2 that dominates and not the other way around. That's not easy because of the barriers that Self 1 has learnt to build up. The gravitas techniques in this book are designed to build awareness first and then a positive action self. That is why most of this book is focused on the doing Self 2 once it has learnt to get the thinking and reflecting out of the way.

You have already completed three of the four steps of Kolb's (1984) learning cycle. In the assessment section you drew on your concrete experiences through a series of questions and reflected on your answers and related these to my model of gravitas. You then drew your conceptual abstraction of what gravitas means to you and when and where you want to focus. The inner coaching team will help you to focus on the right areas to integrate your Self 1 and Self 2 but as yet we haven't introduced the tools and techniques for active experimentation. We have to be careful not to let the inner team overcoach you or you'll end up trying too hard. It's a kind of learning paradox that in order to learn we have to try less hard. Don't tell anyone at school age about this of course.

How do we do this?

- Firstly, rather than always thinking of Self 1 and Self 2 give them each a name – be imaginative.
- Fill your newly named negative Self 1 with images wherever possible. They are more memorable than words. Your brain, body, performance, and public relations coach will thank you for these images rather than bombarding them with instructions.
- Secondly, allow your also newly named Self 2 to get on with it and get into active experimentation. Many of the techniques are somatic so the body is the starting point, and trust your coaching team. Rely on your coaching andragogy to trust in experimental play.
- Thirdly, as the learning process demands that you reflect back on how you did or are doing allow yourself to look at what is really happening in the experiences not judging how well you did. It's time to be less hard on you.

Gallwey suggested that the Self 1 is full of ego and is easily bruised but starts dominating and interferes in performance, so we will have to be careful.

Our inner coaching team has a lot to process. There is a lot of focus on imagery and less on trying too hard. We are also learning that the somatic processes can help build gravitas quickly and effectively rather than think it through all the time. Furthermore, having a visual representation of gravitas in our heads isn't simply an academic exercise, it's a reinforcement of a picture for something that is complex. Therefore, as we move on to tactics and strategies keep the visual model in mind; remember the role models out there for you that help you trigger an understanding of which temperaments matter the most to you. And allow yourself to practice, reflect, and redo as part of the learning process.

Chapter Nine

The Colors of Gravitas: Situational Awareness and Agility

We left the last chapter reflecting on the learning processes we undertake and the enormous job your inner coaching team might have or fortunately might not have. Understanding how the mind can trick us up and how good the body is at teaching the mind helps us achieve the goals we set ourselves become more accessible.

We are going to do a little shape shifting now to help explain the tactics and strategies to build gravitas. Return to the image of the propeller model.

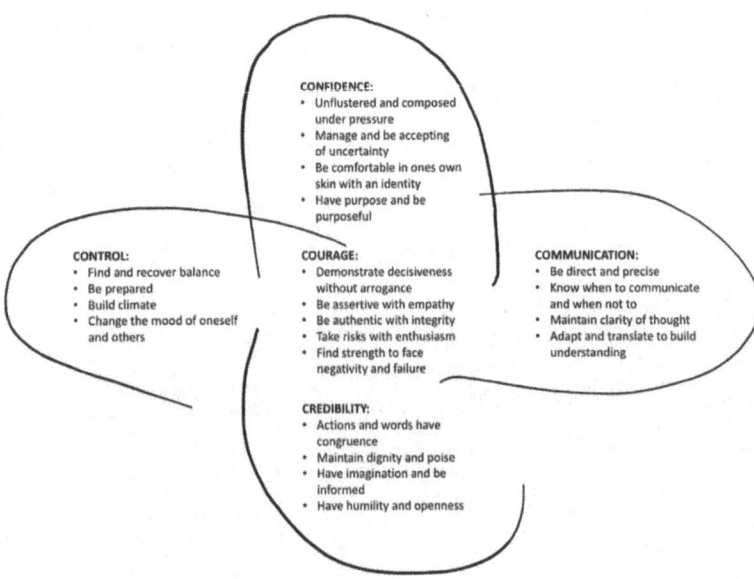

Figure 9.1: The Gravitas Propeller

The Colors of Gravitas: Situational Awareness and Agility

Does it remind you of anything else, especially if we add more of a 3-dimensional tilt to it? Rotate it in your mind so that it now tilts horizontally around the construct of the courage hub. Place a finger under the credibility blade and push down on the confidence blade.

I'm more of a right brain dominant learner but from what I've seen many are not so forgive me and I'll get on with it. The image starts to look a little like planetary rotations. Orbiting around one central force. For me the extra dimension the rotation provides not only adds more movement of the constructs but also situates the constant pull of the forces around not just the central force but also each other. They exist in their own universe, just as we do. Some people's forces are larger than others, understandably, but they represent where we work, live, love, play, and all of those people and situations we encounter.

The first gravitas tactic to learn is to read your universe, and make sense of the situations and environments we encounter. Some of my former colleagues would call this a kind of ecosystem. When I co-developed the gravitas tactics my partners and I focused on finding tools that would quickly allow them to assess how they were behaving and the environments they were in. Environmental and situation reading is the first step in the performing side of developing gravitas. To keep it memorable we use three colors that represent a type of 'temperature.' Although not dissimilar to a traffic light system this focus is more on a kind of heat map and of course there isn't a blue traffic light! Oddly to me the colors are the same as those assigned to quarks in physics but I think I encountered that much later.

Another way to think of the metaphor is of a glass being too full and at risk of overflowing, about right, or too little in the way the expression 'the glass is half full' intends. We used a similar idea in the temperament self-assessment questions, which we will use again in this chapter for more specific situations.

Figure 9.2: The Colors of Gravitas – Glasses

An ideal color is green. The situation and environment are open, engaged, hidden from any type of physical or mental danger, where self-awareness and awareness of others is at its highest point, and there is almost a kind of flow to the interactions with others. The other two colors are red and blue, and indicate a hotter or cooler environment. Red environments indicate more potential danger and that there is a little too much energy circulating, either forcing the situation on your gravitas constructs, or that you are pushing out too much of your own. If it is with a group of people, the atmosphere may appear open, but it is more noisy and full of people pushing their own agendas. Often there is sense that someone or others have a need to be seen to be right. Whereas, at the opposite end in the blue area there is more of an icy feel. Engagement levels are low, and agendas are more quietly hidden, or if not quietly hidden regarded by others more cynically as if everyone is equipped with the red pen of a teacher or auditor looking for errors and judgement. This passive resistance and cynicism are mistakenly seen as a form of intelligence. The red and blue are both challenging in different ways. The bluster and force of the red can be appealing for some and in fact some situations can thrive on it. The energy sucking blue world has its place too as we shall see, but most would find the ideal green to be the most comfortable environment to be it. So, let's break it down into sections and consider examples where there is good and bad.

Universe — Our macro universe is everywhere that we have interactions. At the largest level this includes where we live and work, not in a parochial sense but a geographical sense up to and including the country or countries where we play out our life. It is wherever and with whoever we believe we will need our gravitas to become a strength. For example, when I served in the military in my first proper job my universe wasn't that small despite it being a huge jump from living with my parents. My universe was at the largest level the country for whom I served, the military arm in which I served, and the bases I was stationed. Of course, I travelled on vacations overseas, but this wasn't really my universe where my gravitas orbited. My universe was the armed forces as it dominated my life. It had very strict rules, disciplines, cultures, symbols, rituals, and so did the country in which I lived.

Exercise 1:
- List the places in your universe where you wish your gravitas to develop.
- List the regional or national cultural artefacts I've listed above which have an influence on how your gravitas will play out with others.
- List the work type cultural artefacts that also will have a bearing on your gravitas.

Environment — Your environment is second layer deeper. Now we become more specific about the people you interact with and your more direct sphere of influence or influences. We can add the more recent complication of living and working through a global pandemic. Nearly everyone I have met has found their work practices have changed, often dramatically, and it has changed the orbit of our constructs and consequently how to modify our temperaments.

Exercise 2:
- Within your world of work describe your working environment. If you are entering this practice from a nonwork perspective focus on the living environment.
- How have changes in that environment had an influence on your behavior?
- List which people to whom you wish to be able to demonstrate greater gravitas. Be as extensive as possible. Colleagues, customers, family, friends, even strangers if you need to! Ensure that you add next to the names, the type of person they are, and if strangers — what type of behaviors may inhibit your gravitas?

Situations — This is the third and final stage of building your world. The situations are specific. For example, in the workplace this could be meetings, presenting to seniors, pitches for new work or investors, work social gatherings, leading a team only through digital technology, negotiating, or having confrontational conversations. Outside of work is equally if not more varied but might include parties, attending courses, competing in a sport or leisure pursuits, confronting finance or government officials. For years I worked with acting companies tackling these situations through play and experimentation and we always had the greatest success when clients could be specific. Using your conceptual encounter self-assessment exercise will help here.

Exercise 3:
- List as many situations as you can that are real and granular for you. Note if none of the people were in those situations from the previous list, remove them. Ideally

start with around 20. You can keep coming back to the exercise again and again.
- When you have as many as you can think of, edit them to around half.
- Finally, when you have done that — think of those ten, how many will you be able to immerse yourself in, and practice again and again. Once you have done that cut the list down to around five or six if you can.

I wrote earlier in the book that one of my key clients who was involved in co-developing the gravitas model, when asked, "When is the one situation where you need gravitas?" replied, beautifully and probably accurately, "At a funeral" — and he wasn't an undertaker, and it probably isn't the best situation to practice again and again! However, he was not alone in this thinking as Brett and Kate McKay, in their article profiling Walter Cronkite and his gravitas qualities, state beautifully:

> *Think of a funeral. In such a situation, the man possessing gravitas is able to keep his composure; with compassionate poise, he delivers bad news; with great stamina, he unflaggingly takes care of what needs to be done; with a minister-like mien, he comforts the mourning; with the sagacity of a wise elder, he helps the grieving make sense of what happened. His is the gravitational force that holds people together. His is the healing hand on every shoulder. His is the presence that imparts reassurance and strength, a belief that life will go on. He is a human hearth that people naturally want to gather round.*

A funeral is a blue situation one would hope, but regardless you can also possess gravitas in any context once you recognize the color of the situation and how it connects to people.

The Colors of Gravitas: People

Now that you have the hang of thinking about colors as a way of imaging I am going to add some more detail to the color modeling process. Just as our orbit forces are always moving so do the colors. And not in all cases is a red or blue color bad, and neither is a green color always ideal. Furthermore, they intersect as you can see below within a Venn diagram, rather like the preference pairs of introversion and extroversion, there are two polar extremes and a third mid point, which creates a useful blurring:

Let's look at it a little closer. Whilst the colder blue might be characterized by some of having more negative behaviors and feelings, it also contains positives, as we read in the funeral quote. To be focused, reflective, private, and thoughtful has its place in life. It's a way of getting some privacy, invisibility, and to reenergize. This is where our Myers-Briggs Introvert preferences tend to be more comfortable. The hotter red color similarly contains positives to be energetic, engaging, commanding, and enthusiastic. We don't need to be in the green

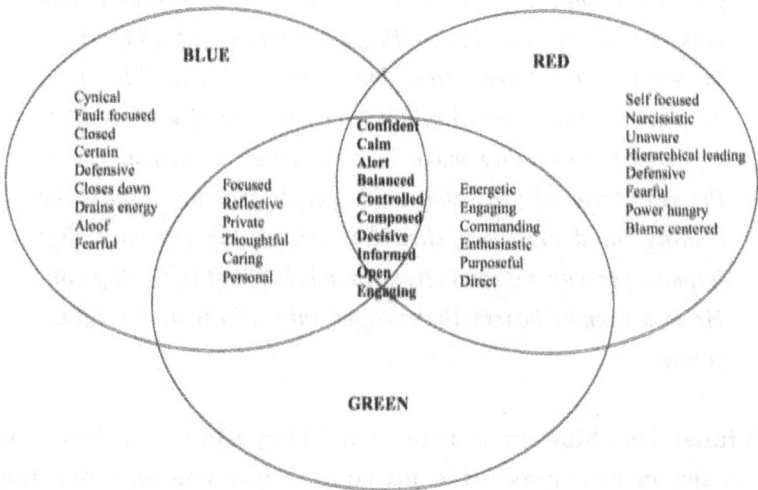

Figure 9.3: The Colors of Gravitas – Positives and Negatives

all the time, because it depends on the color of the situations you encounter and the people you wish to influence. Therefore, when you complete the exercise below, remember that all colors have benefits just like the MBTI types.

Exercise 4:
- Now what we need to do is attach our colors to those people we wish to influence from exercise 2. Either on a computer or on paper find the original list of people and mark a color of red, blue, or green against them.
- If you think that their colors are always changing, I have tended to find that is not the case. Of course, we have some changes but in general tend to be drawn to one, just as we do with our MBTI type. Next to the color add whether the color is in the positive or negative side of the sphere.
- What color would you put next to you? I have often found that people tend to mark themselves as green, because obviously we are perfect. It's all those other people — be honest!
- Lastly, going back to the first exercise, make a record of how the cultural 'norms' you identified could be barriers to the development of your gravitas.

The situational and environmental reading tools are essential first steps within strategies and tactics, and in past practice my students adopted a type of three-color radar constantly scanning the environment and situations rather like 'KITT' the car in the 1980s TV series, *Knight Rider*, feeding back information to the driver. Don't worry if you don't know it, I'm sure you get the image.

I suggest that when you reach this point start to practice the scanning approach. To do so, try to think of yourself in the green color and start to read your internal color radar and ask yourself, how is each environment, person, or situation making me feel about the color I'm in? How it is impacting each of the five constructs? It will be too hard to try to measure the impact on the temperaments at this stage. The color visualization really helps our Self 2 mind to respond quickly to your inner coach.

Using Your Gravitas Reflection Diaries or Journal for Performing

Every time I coach or work for an extended period on the development of gravitas I recommend creating and using a reflection diary or journal. They have been completely effective. The difficulty is committing yourself to doing it and ensuring you complete it in a timely way.

The starting process is to find a method that is easy for you to use. Some of my clients use their phone or tablet. Others create a page on their laptop or desktop, and many still prefer to write it down, but to begin with it's a process of transferring your goals and role models from the gravitas assessment chapter and starting to make general notes that map situations, people and your reactions. Later you can add the actions that you took.

The reason why it's so effective is you can chart progress, which is difficult to recall because in many cases you're trying to change learned reactions and behaviors. But this is also your inner coach's job to start to guide you on when and where you need to develop, and what is effective and ineffective. Your inner coach needs material to work with before the new behaviors become more natural. Using one place to record all of your self-assessment work and practice is the best way if you really want to improve.

Just to give you some examples of client reactions to the journaling, I have included a few elements of their stories below using my journal entries and theirs...

Me: John had enthusiastically debated all of the constructs in the first coaching round and appears to be deeply reflective in nature. He has an air of confidence mentally, but it doesn't always come across somatically. Where he struggled was engaging teams and a style of communication that draws others towards him. He leads and works with large teams of up to 100 people, but often describes the interactions he has as 'red' with a personal desire to behave in the 'green.' In order to increase his gravitas, he primarily should be focusing on three areas: his timing, credibility, and acceptance, stating that:

John: I accepted I couldn't do everything and be in control of every temperament so I broke up the problem and asked pairs of individuals to come back to the next session with a plan.... I learned to not try to control and be involved in every construct and become a bottleneck in decision-making and needed to work out how to capture the feeling of confidence and control based on experience and deliver it in a situation where I don't have the prior experience and would need to extract this from others through coaching.

Me: I felt that John has picked up on his challenge of training to engage others with more experience by being careful not to come across as too confident intellectually, and has managed to read situations and people well. However, his reflection diaries have not yet addressed how to have greater humility, approachability, and to somatically embody confidence to an appropriate level.

Me: Mike has a good sense of self-awareness but has not found it so easy to read others. He describes in a diary entry that:

Mike: I felt more confident following the gravitas session; consequently, easily elevated myself from day-to-day noise onto concentrating on being purposeful by picturing myself being still whilst the noise of the sea thrashes around me.

Me: Mike's main area of focus is to be comfortable with others listening and to set the tone for meeting others, but let others talk so he can steer but get away from the chaos of others.

Me: Rick needs to build an identity he is comfortable with and feed his control.

Rick: The meeting finished 20 minutes early and I felt in control. I had another 'green' situation and I am focused on cultivating my style and look. I hope to keep adding to my credibility. I have already focused on this before but want it to go further and want to try to instill confidence in others as much as myself.

One more challenging diary event related to being in control:

Mike: I was leading a potentially very heated meeting about a stalled project. I became conscious of manipulating the situation by passing energy and emotion at specific times in proceedings to cause a change in thinking.

What was especially interesting is that Mike said:

I felt awkward in the situation and ... I wasn't that pleased how I came over. However, others felt I was being successful and managed the situation effectively.

He described this as perceiving himself as behaving in a 'red' way but being perceived as 'green' and that his own 'discomfort does not necessarily permeate.'

So, you can see the entries are often short, not like a personal diary, and that your inner coach also needs to interpret and write back what is being said as I do as a client coach. In addition, if you leave your entries too long after a situation you will not capture the feeling well enough to make it useful. Try them out and invent your own format.

Chapter Ten

Using the Somatic Embodiment of Gravitas

Earlier in the book I referenced the power of the body as a means of absorbing information and teaching the mind. The power of the body to absorb messages easily beats the mind. When you reflect on those people you wanted to demonstrate your gravitas to you labelled them with a color or perhaps you found you needed more than one, but something told you through your experiences they had a gravitas color. Not everyone will agree with you but that doesn't matter as it is your gravitas that matters. I have met many high energy red MBTI high preference extraverted types who firstly describe themselves as green who are drawn to other reds that those in the blue find abhorrent! Therefore, concentrate on yourself firstly when you assess your thoughts of others. If you recognized yourself as blue and admired the red, you may be in danger of choosing a self-centered person as either a role model or mentor. If you are seeking to transit from the extreme of blue or red often the actual move is not as great as it may seem. If you have had the courage to describe yourself as an extreme blue on the left then you have acknowledged that perhaps you tend to be cynical, internally harsh on others, suspicious, don't listen as well as you know you should, and may consider yourself a proud introvert. Any adjustments you make can be quite small to you but have a profound effect on others. Your introverted self needs to only use its skills to improve focus on others, be more reflective before making judgements, and be kinder to yourself. Effectively your inner coach recognizes that your dominant Self 1 type thinking tends to override your Self 2 which is more somatically oriented.

Coaching yourself to trust your Self 2 type isn't a quick learning process to develop into a habit, but it is quick in terms of the effect on the brain. It quietens the mind.

Exercise 1:
- Find some video footage of people speaking to a group, ensuring you pick at least ten people talking in very different situations. For example, you might choose a TED talk, a political briefing, a business presentation, an awards ceremony, a *Shark Tank* or *Dragons' Den* type of business idea pitch, or post sports event interview, or an arts documentary. Whatever you prefer.
- Ideally you need to find someone speaking where you can see the whole of their body rather than someone leaning against a lectern.
- Turn the sound off initially and watch them for around five minutes.
- Make a note in your journal of what you observe — concentrate on the whole of the body not just the face.
- Which color do you sense they are and why?

Somatic Guidance and Observations

Many of us reading will have or have had pets or animals in our lives. Most have at least encountered one directly. Animals communicate with us and each other without a language we recognize although sometimes they are vocal, and we can almost guess what they are trying to say. But they are often responding to our cues. Dogs and cats are probably the most common pets, and I'll use dogs as an example.

All animal senses are much more highly attuned than ours. We do use ours too but it's not often until we lose one that it really hits home how much we value it. As I am writing this my wife has been diagnosed with Covid-19 for a second time, and yet again she has lost her sense of taste and smell. It

Using the Somatic Embodiment of Gravitas

happened to me a few months earlier, and if you too have ever experienced it, it is the strangest feeling. When we go to eat something, our brain anticipates what the taste and smell will be. It begins with the sense of smell, the most powerful of all senses, that directly links to our memory and reaction center in the prefrontal cortex. When there is no receptor for smell immediately the taste seems odd. When the taste goes, all there is left is the physical sensation.

Similarly, when we shut the sound off we rely on our observation and intuition. Our sense of touch, smell, and taste are outside, but it requires real focus to observe someone completely for five minutes, so our intuition fills in some of the gaps too. Those with more of a preference for intuition may find this process more natural initially, but those with a preference for sensing (go back to your MBTI for help if you need reminding) are good at picking up on details, but because you can do both it just requires more practice to blend both functions and improve your observation. When you move to live observations your other senses will kick back in of course.

What did you observe? Did you look at the face first, or the whole body, did you get to see them walk on to stage, did you notice the walking style, their hands, their fingers, the head angle, their shoulders, their style, their eyes, their lips, their speed of movement? On the more intuitive side did you get a sense of tension, relaxation, their breathing, or something else?

That's a lot to observe. I have conducted live classes with professional adults, and when I asked someone in the room, the kind of answers I have had a range from the one-liners:

"He seemed tall."
"I liked her dress."
"Nice shoes."

To the more useful:

> "They seemed to know what they are talking about and looked comfortable."
> "I can't say why but I felt warmed to them, I could see them smiling but it wasn't all the time, it's as if they use the smile to connect and pause."

The difference sometimes has been as simple as those with a sensing preference at the extreme, stating specifics, compared to the intuitive extreme providing more of a sense of the person, their physiological state, and their relationship with others. However, what we need to look for is more specific than either set of examples, and goes back to the pet dog example.

I used to watch a TV program called the *Dog Whisperer* by Cesar Millan. Whether you have seen the show and like or dislike it doesn't matter because the overall message is pretty simple. He aims to get a dog into a passive, attentive, calm, and submissive state. He tended to work with dogs who were the opposite of this, of course, but his observations on the somatic nature of dogs is relevant. We are bound together like dogs with a musculoskeletal system with common features such as two eyes, two ears, one nose, legs (four would be useful sometimes), one heart, one tail. And so on. Hang on — I said one tail. Well in a way we all do, and I'll explain. When a dog gets into a particular emotional state such as fear, anxiety, excitement, aggression, or calmness, the body and brain in synchronicity create a physical reaction. The fear and anxiety state creates an observable tension. With aggression there is a stillness and focus, with the eyes fixated, and a body that can be seen as ready to spring. With excitement there is an accompanying wiggle at the rear, a lowering at the front legs, and so on. But the one area that really gives away the emotional state is the tail, or in the case of a docked tail, what is left. Cesar Millan will sometimes physically move the position of the tail and then observe a change in the emotional state, but more importantly he ensures his body is in a calm state, as we often mirror that of others. Now we don't have a tail that we can see (except in the movie Shallow Hal!) but we have something called a tail bone. When we are tense our tail bone starts to look like it is tucking under like the tail of a dog curling between its legs. It might appear to go rigid with our back and our glutes — you will be able to feel it. Of course, those with other physical issues such as back pain or severely tight hamstrings will also find that tension pulling our tail, but it is one of the first clues of somatic emotional state. Did you see any clues as to the tail bone state of your people in the videos? It was probably difficult to see but I want you to begin to become aware of your emotional state and tail bone tension. When we can learn to move our tail bone through somatic adjustment, breathing changes, and other relaxation techniques, we can begin to alter our mental state rather than think our way through it. This is where Self 2 can teach Self 1 to quieten down. In fact, as noted by Bill Bryson in his book, *A Short History of Nearly Everything*, he writes that in fact we have the same DNA as a mouse to grow a tail. It's not a pleasant image.

Let's move to other physical actions. When we observe someone walking onto a stage or to the front of a room to speak, more cues about the 'state' are provided. I recall one piece of video footage showing a very well-known public figure almost jogging, with long strides, onto the stage before beginning to speak at an event. But it wasn't a jog of, 'I can't wait,' it was one of, 'I need to move.' When we build a state of anxiety the body fuels itself with unwanted chemicals through our adrenal glands which are helpful when we need to spring into action, but whilst we wait for an event to occur and we are static are unhelpful. Remember, this is the body's 'fight or flight' response. The clues about the anxiety state of this particular person were a combination of three things. The springy, jog-like leap to the stage was a physical release, which indeed the body does need in an anxious, or much worse, panic state, but you could also see the person gasping as they were about to speak and 'wringing' their hands in anticipation. Now this isn't rocket science and is very common in situations where someone is about to speak in public; it is what we notice in others before a single word is said, and it creates an equally anxious response in us. When we move to the section on communication, I always remind those who are anxious about speaking that almost everyone in an audience does not want you to fail. They want you to do well as it also helps them relax.

So, did you notice any of those physical cues in the videos you watched? I have referred to what you would not be able to see in the video as the unfortunate presenter's Self 1 completely dominating their Self 2, and telling them with self-critique: "You're in trouble, you need to get out of here, you're going to screw this up," and the Self 2 responding in physiological panic.

The next observation point is about the sense of weight, of gravity. Very important when we are talking about gravitas of course. When the body is in an anxious state I have already pointed out that it needs to move to balance the adrenaline and cortisol flooding the system. When you see someone starting to speak you can continue to sense this state of anxiety, which can have different energy responses depending on whether the person speaking is on the extremes of the red or the blue colors. With high level anxiety the sense of gravity reduces, leaving the body feeling light or even weightless and the feet in particular almost feel like they're floating. During observation you will see a constant shifting or tapping of the feet. In itself that is neither a red nor a blue response, but it is certainly not green. I will explain how to counter this effect when we move to specific tips, but at the moment I want to raise your awareness. Those speaking from the far right of the red zone move more vigorously, use their arms more expressively, and more quickly than the far left of the blue zone person that uses something to hang on to, so they don't float away. Furthermore, you would notice the blue speaker is touching their neck and their face more.

The other two physical points in my video example were the gasping and the use of hands, and I'll begin with the latter. The hands provide a massive clue but also an opportunity for Self 2 to teach Self 1 (remember you may have given your two selfs names to personalize them) to be quiet. Grasping, wringing, and hiding of the hands is a very natural anxious response but you may also notice in some of your videos that trained speakers or presenters use their hands especially well. One favored technique is to temple the fingers and thumbs with the hands at the center of the body near the belly. It's a steadying technique that is calming internally and reassuring externally. It can't be done excessively as it looks manufactured and is similarly matched by the cradling of hands which also works well in a seated position. You may have noticed on whatever viewing platforms that you use for news, current affairs, entertainment type discussion shows, and so on that there has been a move away from the classic sitting behind a desk only showing the trunk and head of the speaker with no sign that they have legs or hands. And if their hands did suddenly appear it was most distracting. This is on purpose. Even where they have desks you often see the camera draw back to show to whole set and more of the whole person and their hands. So, you now get a more complete picture. Presenters sitting on stools and sofas are more common and so therefore is our exposure to their entire somatic state. Ironically, now we are in whatever stage we are of the post Covid-19 pandemic world restructure, many of us that still work from home or are involved in long-distance interactions are stuck with the former body and headshot only image, which is rather outdated.

There is also something that you will not notice on a video, but you can observe in yourself. The palms can provide a clue to the oxygenation in the body. That is, how well you are breathing. I can guarantee if you could see the person I referred to as gasping, that their breathing was shallow, and poisoning their bloodstream with alkaline as they gasped to get air in, and they exhaled very little out for a considerable time beforehand. By the time they are about to speak they are in a dire physiological state. If you were to look at their palms they would look blotchy with pale dots and pink, from their fingertips to the wrist. As I have said, this is something you can observe in yourself but unfortunately when and if you do see it, it will not help to get out of it as all it will do is fuel the Self 1 that something is wrong, and it is going to get worse. As an introvert who has suffered from extreme panic attacks all my life, and who has had to speak publicly for almost all their professional life, I know this is very real. But it is also possible to learn how to manage it.

The final point you may have observed in the hands is linked to their use in movement and in touching. Unless the people you watched were hanging on to dear life from a lectern you may notice how often they touch their face and neck. When we observe it live we often copy it, and it makes us feel uneasy because their nervousness becomes ours as well. Trained presenters learn to avoid it through practice, observation, reflection, and re-practice. The animal link reappears here again. Instinctively when a dog or cat with a litter wants to pick up one of their offspring it will pick them up by the scruff of the neck. Even when they are older if you massage the top of a dog's neck it is reassuring to them. Our necks feel vulnerable but also a reassuring sense of home. When we touch it, we are saying one of two things. I'm trying to reassure myself or I need to go home. Either way it is a sense of anxiety.

A further breathing state observation you can make alongside gasping and gulping is observed through the shoulders and chest. The need to oxygenate more is accompanied by shoulder shrugging and chest pumping. It's often quite subtle but the person in the blue situational color is doing it more obviously than the person in the red. The red person is too busy talking and moving!

The last of your somatic observation guides is to do with the head. More especially the angle of the head. This is not the left and the right tilt, rather it's the pointing angle of the chin. The self-orientated, self-important far right of the red zone often is accompanied with a tilt of the chin upwards. It is as if to say I'm more important than you. It mustn't be confused with a simple height difference, but those same people actually walk around like that most of the time. Be careful when you observe this at home! In the acting world I have seen this taught as status positions. Not looking down at notes is not to be confused with the blue zone, but never looking up at the audience is. Start to notice this in yourself, and be careful to develop and culture a horizontal gaze that looks towards everyone, not staring. The eyes give us a clue to our overall mental state. They actually hold a tension that might be difficult to observe in others unless they dart quickly from side to side. At times if you experience this eye darting it can be a very distracting train of thought that makes you feel like your inner coach has become obsessed with Self 1 self-talking about where to look, just as it can do with the rest of the body and ends up being a mechanical mess. However, there is a sensation that can have a profound effect on relaxing the whole body that centers on the eyes and is accompanied by Self 2 focused talk, telling yourself to "relax behind the eyes." It's very effective.

Exercise 2:
- Now play the videos with the sound on.
- What do you notice about the voice?
- Does this change the color zone you first chose, and if so why?

The voice, how we communicate, and what we say is often the connection that most of us have with another person. Certainly, the previous exercise is asking you to tune in to other senses but if you are able to hear a voice it is hard to switch it off like you can in the recordings. You have probably heard yourself speak on a recording and almost everyone I have worked with who isn't a trained speaker, actor, or presenter finds hearing their voice uncomfortable. It even has a label — voice confrontation. It often doesn't quite fit the sound we think that others hear. Sometimes even the accent sounds different. There are some good reasons for this.

Firstly, most of us don't get to hear ourselves as others do as it is not part of our daily world of work. It may not even matter or bother you. Secondly, and this is more somatic, our mouth, ears, and brain are all pretty close to each other. What we hear directly from a very small distance from where the voice starts is conducted and resonates through our bones providing us with what sounds like a deeper richer tone than the voice others hear. As a result, it sounds weird to us when we listen to a recording of ourselves. Furthermore, research has been conducted on what types of voices we like hearing, and it will not surprise you that deeper richer tones are more appealing. In fact, Sheffield University in the UK conducted a study to find out which voices were most appealing, and found in the world of film, TV, and radio that Jeremy Irons, Alan Rickman, Judi Dench, Honor Blackman, and the broadcaster Mariella Frostrup had the ideal combination of depth of tone, speed of speech, the number of words per minute, and the time of each pause. The ideal was described as no more than 164 words per minute and no less than 0.48 seconds for pauses! It sounds very formulaic and it was; just as it was also very UK centric. Another found that legendary US broadcaster Walter Cronkite had the ideal voice to convey gravitas with a sound that created a sense of confidence and sufficient knowledge with a speed of just 124 words per minute. There are plenty of other excellent books on developing voice for communication and I don't intend to try and replicate all of their knowledge here but have practiced with clients and students to try to adjust speed, breath, and pause to build gravitas. And we can do the same very easily here.

Exercise 3:
- Choose a speech either from a web search or I used a book of great speeches from around the world.
- Set up a means of recording yourself, which is pretty easy of course these days.
- Read from the speech for five minutes.
- Replay the speech and count the number of words you speak in a minute and compare them to the supposed ideal.
- Remember that because you are doing the exercise after reading this and you may not know the speech well, you will naturally be slower than normal.
- Now, identify a presentation you have given before and try giving it again to your recording device, even if it includes presentation slides.
- Is there a difference?

On the whole I have found that most of my clients speak too quickly, and as pressure and anxiety increase, the speeds increase again. We will cover the art of presenting with gravitas in a little more detail but the main learning point is not to worry about the number of words you speak but to focus on the pauses between sentences, using your breath as if you're a metronome, helping you to keep your mind clear to maintain clarity of thought, and to help ensure that others have time to absorb the points you wish to land with those you are speaking to.

As we explore situations you will encounter to develop your gravitas it will appear again as a clear tip for you to practice, but as you are reading now, "relax behind the eyes," and see how it affects any tension in the body and your breathing.

In summary we have focused these two opening sections on reading the environment and situations by attaching a color zone and have understood hopefully that all the color zones can be useful, but we will need to be careful stepping into the extremes of the blue and red. In addition, we have begun to try and attach colors to those we are hoping to build our gravitas with. However, when we practice attaching colors to people without a voice our focus switches to using our somatic senses so that it tones down our judgement from what people say and how they say things. Hopefully the somatic guidance has raised your awareness of the vast range of cues bodies give to emotional states, and how these relate to our color reading. And finally, although we have to be cautious about judging everyone and every situation, we can apply these to our own feelings about how we sense our preferred zones and what we may be providing as cues to others.

Chapter Eleven

Situations: Strategies and Tactics Part One – People

In the final section I have selected a variety of popular or perhaps unpopular situations that people face. Then we can leverage the knowledge and strategies that we've covered thus far and bring in some new approaches to develop gravitas from the unique perspectives of introverts.

Primarily I have written this book to help understand why any gravitas we do have sometimes disappears especially in the more extroverted world of work. However, despite the overall interest for the more introverted it is also relevant for extroverts because the extreme end of extroversion is a dangerous state that needs to be reeled in in order to attain effective gravitas. I also wanted to stress that for some it isn't as simple as one is introverted or extroverted at all times. For many it can feel more of a continuum dependent on situations that moves around just as the constructs of gravitas do. And that is a good thing. There is no magic fix but there is an inner coach in us that can be highly effective at quietening down our critical side or self-important side by focusing on imagery, mental and role modeling, and the process of observation, reflection, practice, reflection, and re-practice. Lastly, I felt it was important to reference a theoretical approach to demonstrate how gravitas might work, and how it differs from other qualities because that helps us to build our self-awareness and bespoke approach to personal development.

Many of the same tactics cross over regardless of the situation, but how you employ them will be dependent on the color zone of the environment and the people involved. Not all of the five constructs and temperaments will have equal importance.

The world of work is the place where many of us spend the majority of our awake adult lives, and it has changed dramatically recently and continues to do so. The work landscape covers a huge array of situations, cultures, politics, personalities, agendas, dreams, and stress. Let's introduce five key work scenarios:

1. Leading teams and meetings
2. Influencing peers
3. Influencing the boss
4. Social engagements
5. Presentations

The first four are very much focused on the people aspect of leading. Part two has a chapter solely focused on presentations addressing the self-management of anxiety, and the impact aspect of structure and delivery. I can think of many more, but these are the most frequent types of situations that students, clients, and participants have asked me to work with for many years, and actually arc across a huge variety of human interactions in the workplace. Each situation is structured in the following way. Firstly, an introduction to the type of situation with an example. Secondly, how to read the environment and use the color zone approach to build imagery of the situation and the people that might matter as well as know yourself. And finally, tactics to employ and practice. After we have covered each of the five situations, I will ask you to reevaluate your goals from the section on "Knowing Your Gravitas" and to go and work on which tactics and tips to try back in your workplace. It is also important for me to stress this isn't supposed to be a section detailing all the approaches to managing and leading. This solely focuses on gravitas, when it is most needed, why it is difficult to obtain, and how effective it will be with practice.

Leading Teams and Meetings

Leading other people is one of the most challenging parts of either rising the corporate ladder or running your own business. It can be immensely rewarding but for many the process of getting to a point where leading others is pleasurable can be very painful and exhausting. Even when a stage might be reached where everything is going well that position doesn't stay for long as people leave, environments shift, and we may indeed move on. However, again let's remind ourselves that this isn't a book on how to lead teams or businesses, it is about building our individual gravitas with those we wish to influence, and finding accessible memorable ways in which to be able to do so in practice. In addition, to the broad focus of leading people I simply couldn't leave out the dreaded curse on leadership time, meetings.

I have got to the stage in my career as a self-employed consultant and coach where thankfully meetings feature much less than they used to. Furthermore, when you work for yourself you become much more focused on making sure that what you do adds value rather than just keeps everyone and the proverbial pet dog informed.

The journey from being a lone contributor to a team member to one leading others is an enormous one. Managing and then leading a team is quite daunting initially. Suddenly you have to keep everyone busy, let go of previous duties, monitor and develop performance. And often all of this is done within the constraints of how performance and development are 'allowed' to be done.

Meetings, meetings, and more meetings. As you climb or have climbed up they dominate more and more of any time you have. I recall when I worked for a global consulting firm that they would probably occupy as much as 80% of the usual working time. As a result to make up for the 'lost' time I had dig into later and later hours to catch up with all the work that needed to be done directly as a result of the new tasks and goals set at those meetings! And then there is the difference between leading a meeting either with your own team or teams or more often cross team meetings with others, and simply attending someone else's meeting. As we consider the complexities of meeting roles two further dimensions appear. Time and preparedness. From a time perspective depending on the culture of the organization, back-to-back meetings pose huge problems as diaries get filled from one direct hour to the next. And location to location. In large places you might find yourself almost running from one side of a building to another, or another building. Leading to the opening phrase often heard, "Sorry I'm late," or if you're leading a meeting having to send the message, "Sorry – we are running ten minutes behind." Even with remote working running late for meetings continues as previous meetings might overrun and/or you run into 'technical difficulties'! From a preparedness perspective one meeting leading to another continuously depletes preparedness, and both create the look of a person in a rush.

So, let's begin with your preparation. At the beginning of each day go through the same routine. Hopefully you won't have ten meetings requiring gravitas each day.

Situation:
- Is this a gravitas meeting from my perspective, and if so why?
- Who do I need to demonstrate my gravitas to?
- Which constructs and temperaments do I need to be at a level four or five?
- Who are my role model people for each of the five constructs? — It could just be one.

Pretty simple start as all the situation questions will begin with the same macro tone.

Environment:
- What is the situation color?
- Which color zone is/are the person/people I need to influence?
- What zone am I in?

Tactics:
The tactics will contain a series of visual and somatic cues given to you by your inner coach to help you teach Self 1 to be quiet, and practical tips for some of the more common constructs and temperaments that are needed to get you as close to the green zone as possible, but it will depend initially on the situation zone.

Situation Goals: If your meeting is in a red zone you may aim to cool it down. It depends on the nature of the meeting. For example, I recall watching a creative meeting with the members of the band Metallica. It was chaotically loud, funny, moody, and exciting. Completely red, but it suited what they were trying to achieve creatively! I've also led brainstorming meetings for a few hours and the red zone seemed about right until we needed to actually get down to some precise actions and therefore move into the green zone, but either way the radar was always on. If it is a typical serious blue zone meeting, you may be required to lift it. You may need to move yourself to red to inject some energy if required before returning it to the green. Remember what gravitas and its connection to gravity means. You have to create a greater mass of energy to match the mass you are trying to move. When it is only you and you are leading a large group of others you have to match their total mass and more to move it.

Role Model: Which one/ones do you have in mind? – Visualize them.

Tail Bone and Movement: Firstly, be conscious of how you hold yourself. Where is the tension? As you walk to the meeting try 'standing with the weight in your hips.' Say it to yourself over and over. Do you feel yourself walking almost straight-legged and from the hip, or using your whole body? Relax in the hips as you walk. Finally — have a role model in mind who you think walks well. Personally, I used Richard Gere but that might not be for everyone!

Breathing: Check your palms; if you have a chance and can check in a mirror look at yourself, check the tail bone again and see if you can move it backwards a tiny bit by relaxing your glutes. Breathe counting in to 4 seconds, hold for 5, and out for 7. This might be difficult to do during meetings.

Seating: If you can choose a place visible to all where you are more central to the orbit of others. This is essential if you are leading. Whilst seated discreetly place one hand on your belly and focus your breathing to stop yourself breathing heavily through your chest. Feel the belly move in and out. You can cradle your hands below the table if you don't need to be the attention but when you do need to move them above the table slowly.

Eyes: Relax behind them, and look and breathe around the room, especially towards those you wish to have more gravitas with.

Jaw: Press the tip of your tongue to the roof of your mouth gently just behind your teeth. Often you won't realize how much you might have a tight jaw or be grinding your teeth.

Constructs and Temperaments: Your personal temperaments you wish to focus on are of course unique to you and your situation. However, common ones I encounter when coaching others are:

- Be unflustered and composed (confidence)
- Have a purpose and be purposeful — this creates direction (confidence)
- Know when to communicate and when not to (communication)

- Be prepared (control)
- Build climate, be intentional about the climate you want (control)

These cover the constructs of confidence, communication, and control as an example but for you perhaps you might need to dip into the other two constructs of courage and credibility.

When concentrating on color movement and your somatic reading of yourself and others, you are already using your Self 2 visual skill to make progress. Being unflustered requires use of breathing but also try to create an image of yourself being grounded whilst others around you seem to be rotating. Having one overall purpose will help build confidence as well, but the timing of when you speak is critical. Using your hands and editing your contribution, the attention focuses on you, and finally, especially if you are leading — choose the climate you want as part of your preparedness and have it written down in front of you, so it doesn't leave your mind as part of imagery.

Influencing Peers

This section is broken into two equal parts of influencing: your peers and your boss. They share in common a lack of personal positional power and require a lot of emphasis on the construct of control supported by each of the other four.

One of the unique challenges especially as we work increasingly with flatter organizations, cross functionally, and less hierarchical is building personal gravitas without power, especially with peers. Your overall MBTI preferences provide a very good starting point in terms of how you might be seen by others and some potential blind spots, but with gravitas this is more delicate. With peers more than any other group the danger of arrogance and lack of empathy are more real, and they are hard to recover from. Also, it can be hard having your voice heard so finding gravitas becomes essential.

Unlike the meeting situation you are not working with specific events (although you might be if that is the scenario where you wish to build gravitas) but probably ongoing relationships. There are also other areas of complication. A peer group may not be as equal as it seems. There are perceived power differences and then profession perceptions. The corporate lawyers may see themselves as better than another group, the human resources people may be sneered at by another; if you're a journalist in a media company, an engineer in an engineering company, or a doctor in a hospital you are likely to have a significant power advantage. It can be even worse if there's an external consulting group involved because they probably see themselves as above everyone! A political minefield.

Situation:
- Who do I wish to demonstrate my gravitas to?
- Which constructs and temperaments do I need to be at a level four or five?

Environment:
- What is the general operating environment zone color?
- Which people operate in the blue or red zones?
- What zone am I?

Tactics:
The somatic tactics remain somewhat the same as in situation 1. However, depending on the peers you are trying to build gravitas with you may need to adapt for each person. However, unlike meetings you are in effect always on display, so each day is a process of check my physicality, pay attention to my breath, and ensure when I am dealing with those I am focused on so that I always know which temperaments are the most important.

From an introverted perspective this can be difficult when dealing with red zone peers especially if they have superiority complex. If you are introverted with shyness, which isn't always the case, there are some steps to work on.

- Firstly, associate yourself not with shyness but your uniqueness.
- Shut your Self 1 judgmental and critical voice down and think of your strong points.
- Deal with activities and conversations up front by speaking early.
- Remember others may not see you as shy, perhaps just quiet — use it as a strength as there is a lot of gravitas in 'less is more' if you recall the earlier chapters.
- Don't ghost away in encounters. Always leave by saying something.
- Maintain dignity and poise somatically as this will improve your credibility.

Constructs and Temperaments:

Many of the common temperaments are:
- Be comfortable in your own skin and identity (confidence)
- Change the mood of yourself and others (control)
- Be assertive with empathy (courage)
- Actions and words have congruence — be aware of your leadership shadow (credibility)
- Have humility and openness (credibility)

To recap, the constructs at play here are confidence, control, courage, and credibility.

The blue zone introvert can actually play very well in this space as an empathetic and thoughtful listener, but they need to find comfort in themselves. The congruence of actions and words builds trust through the equation. Remember? Credibility + Reliability + Intimacy + Self Orientation.

Influencing the Boss

Pretty much everyone wants to influence their boss, and to do so with gravitas if it's not a threat to them is an ideal. If you are the 'boss' your job is not only to lead with gravitas but instill it in others. This last point is very important. Real gravitas leadership has the capacity and skill to pass it on to others.

I've had some pretty terrible bosses actually, ranging from one who used to ensure he was always at work before everyone came in and left after them only to chastise their team (or group as is more likely) members for not doing the same. Another who only talked about themselves, and another who never seemed to be around but always said they were available. Another who firmly believed and stated that any success was down to them. So-called 'open door' leaders with their office door firmly closed at most times. Bosses who love to espouse how leadership should be done but leading organizations that behave in the complete opposite way. I've seen cost cutting focused CEOs despised by everyone but always tell everyone else that their focus is growth. And perhaps the worst of all, inevitably, the boss bullies. One boss of mine liked coming up to me and saying regularly, "You know I pay more in tax each month than you earn in a year" — seriously! We have also in the last few years seen quite a few of the very top CEOs holding company 'Zoom' meetings lacking complete empathy in people stuck in tiny apartments, struggling with technology, trying their best to contribute, whilst being told they need to do more and shouldn't expect the comfy relationship with their home office to last. And for many it hasn't.

Nevertheless, there are lots of very good ones and hopefully you are to. I have had some pretty decent ones too, however, and I am mindful that I have been one for many years and for a few different companies. I've made my fair share of errors and these stick in my mind permanently. The process of influencing your gravitas is not as difficult as with peers, and it will leave you being comfortable with who you are. However, be warned. If you have a hierarchically close red zone boss, they are not your friend and the best you can do is work on your constructs in the green zone. Do not try to equal their red zone behavior with the same color — it may be an equal and opposite reaction on paper, but it isn't when the power variable is considered.

Situation:
- Do you need gravitas with your boss?
- What is the culture like in the business they lead?
- Does the culture need to change and what is your role?

Environment:
- What zone are they in?
- How do you think they would describe the zone you're in?
- What temperaments do you think they would want you to develop?
- Which role models do you have for those temperaments?
- Which temperaments are important for you to improve?

Tactics:

Always stay green! That may sound simple, but it depends on where they and you are. If your boss is described as green and you are too then you already have sufficient gravitas, I would hope. If, however, you are blue and they are green, the tactics of the more introverted in the previous section apply.

Constructs and Temperaments:

Common temperaments are:
- Be authentic with integrity (courage)
- Be direct and precise (communication)
- Take risks with enthusiasm (courage)

- Be comfortable in one's own skin and identity (confidence)
- Be prepared (control)

The constructs of confidence, communication, courage, and control are all at work in this situation. Although I placed 'be prepared' at the bottom of the list, it is the golden gravitas temperament when dealing with the boss. It is not necessary to know everything, but preparation is key. Having an authentic identity which represents your integrity is also essential as you do not want to end up a clone of your boss, but it takes courage to do so. Time is also often limited when it comes to spending time to influence your boss, so being direct and precise with edited communication is powerful. If you are trying to get noticed in meetings or conversations focus on your breath to create space for you to think and speak, even if it creates uncomfortable pauses, and be prepared to use the risk temperament to speak your mind and sometimes focus on saying the unexpected. These final 2 points are vital because if you read and recall earlier my research found that senior leaders were looking for more from the construct of courage from those further down the power distance ladder.

Social Engagements

Around ten years ago I took on a coaching client and I'll refer to him as Don for his anonymity. Don was around 50 years old enjoying a successful career, but there was one aspect of his professional life he abhorred: social engagements. He was married to an equally successful partner but one who was as confidently extroverted as much as Don's introversion was extreme. She worked as a diplomat and social skills were a requirement and social events an almost weekly activity, and much to Don's constant dread he was often expected to attend. His interest in gravitas coaching revolved almost entirely around his lack of confidence in social settings. I recall him saying almost right up front, "I just don't get small talk, what's the point?" He would go on to ask, "What do people actually talk about?" It's something that I have heard over and over again, and I've witnessed just how uncomfortable some people are, especially when I would run week-long residential courses where built into the design format was a need to socially participate in evening activities. I too would usually have to accompany participants in those activities, and as another introvert I didn't always look forward to them either.

Some corporate clients would look at a five-day course design, calculate how many waking hours there would be, and then try and fill nearly all of them. All of us on the delivery side knew all too well that was a mistake, but that didn't make much of a difference. And so, on the morning of the first day when I would run through the itinerary, I could visibly see the look on the faces of the introverts as total horror. Fortunately, I hope they could sense my empathy with them, and I always was up front with them about the challenges they would face. Well, Don's type of fear would generally be the same as 50% of any large group I had facilitated. It was not only just a fear of social engagement, but a major source of anxiety and energy depletion.

Introverts need much more private recovery from extroverted activity. When forced to attend a residential development course the constant extroverted learning environment is overstimulating, and just when it seems that a day is over the dreaded group meals and evening activities leave no room for the introverted to retreat and recharge, alone!

And so, it was with Don. After a week working in his extroverted world, leading teams, projects, and meetings, the last thing he wanted to do was accompany his wife to a work social party. Therefore, I set him some homework, which we shall cover here.

Situation:
- Describe how you are feeling before the party.
- What is your greatest fear?

Environment:
- Describe the color zone of the party.
- How do you want others to see you at the party?

Tactics:

As with all of our situations the first tactic is to focus on the somatic preparation. Where there is anxiety prior to the social engagement there is of course tension. The physical tension will be felt as always through our core and glutes, and in turn our breathing becomes labored, almost conscious, and more rapid. Once those physiological cues get a hold, our Self 1 rears its head and begins to self-critique.

The somatic preparation begins with creating an image of how you wish to appear at the party. Moving effortlessly, almost gliding around a room, smiling, listening with just a handful of people hanging on to your every word before joining another group. At the end a confident farewell, leaving just a little early with many waves and cheerios echoing inside your head and around the room.

The reality for Don when he reported back was quite different. He remained tense and self-conscious throughout the evening. His wife left his side early leaving him clinging to a corner of the room, champagne in one hand, nervously grinning with the hope someone would speak to him but in fact he found himself standing next to a group of four, listening in without contributing. After checking his watch for the twentieth time and counting down the few hours by looking at his wife to say, it's time we left, and he then ghosted out of the room at an exhausting 10:30.

And therefore, the next time we concentrated on getting his visual image right by concentrating on the first tactic — positioning.

Don's orbit was right on the outer fringes of his universe inside the room. He had noticed he always stood near to an exit and seemed to be trotting to the bathroom, not because he needed to but just because he needed to move and sometimes hide. Therefore, I asked him to move more towards the center of a room. Before he did this, I asked him to use a technique that Patsy Rodenburg (2007) described in her book on *Presence*. He was told to pause as he entered the room and breathe towards the four corners of the room, a technique incidentally that works well with presenting too. The breathing is subtle but measured, and after grabbing his drink move to join a group and simply say 'good evening' and introduce himself. The longer he left those introductions the more the anxiety and self-consciousness would grow. You don't have to lead a conversation, but you have to be physically in it. You are included when you are there. For example, I remember once leading a course on executive presence in South Africa for a mining company, and the culture of the company there was that people would get up and leave constantly, take phone calls and have private conversations. They had asked for a course on presence, but the irony was infuriating. So, eventually I slammed a book on the table at the front and loudly stated, "You can't have presence if you are simply not present." "How do you think your teams feel if every moment you get distracted and wander off?" It was a cultural difference, but the point landed well. I had that same experience just once before whilst teaching in Qatar to a local all-male leadership group. The men would wander in late and then drift out without comment, spend many minutes gossiping with neighbors, and then eventually concentrate for five minutes before off they'd go again. There are understandably lots of cultural norms at play here. But, you have to be present to at least obtain presence; you need also to contribute to build confidence, and ultimately attain and share gravitas.

Therefore, after focusing on somatic imaging and breathing, move to a more central orbit. The construct of courage is the most powerful at play for the introverted in social situations, and represents the sun in our star and planetary model metaphor. Speaking early is the next thing to focus on, and the structure of a conversation. I borrowed a four-part socializing strategy from Dr. Marti Olsen Laney. As part of small talk, you have to:

1. Rehearse and learn 'openers'
2. Learn to keep a conversation going with 'sustainers'
3. Know how to master 'transitions'
4. Always use 'closers'

Don's scientific logical mind liked the idea of small talk structures. He could analyze where he was in a conversation, and that there could be a way out. But before the way out — a way in. This is why I would role model with him how to greet people and introduce himself. He had never really done that before because he said whichever group he joined were always mid-conversation. But he did admit it was more awkward saying nothing and if he didn't say anything it was too late to suddenly announce himself, so he would tend to listen then try and find another group by ghosting out and ideally find another lone introvert to ambush. And so, he had his opener. A simple "Good evening," "I'm Don, Sarah's (not her real name either) husband." And not to be afraid to offer at some point "that I do find these engagements a little tough without being a fluent talker." You'll nearly always find someone who agrees and then you're up and running.

The sustainers are easy. They're just questions. If you've announced yourself, you can always ask, "What conversation have I just found my way in to?" Eventually someone will hopefully ask you a question and that will ease the anxiety. Introverts are generally good listeners so use those skills and take comfort in your identity as one. Transitions are subject shifters, and it is always the skill of the listener to find the gaps to move a transition. The last one is as important as the first because you must not fade away. Have a close. It might be, "Oh excuse me — I've just seen someone I need to talk to," or "I think my partner has given me the nod — please excuse me I need to go and talk to them." And eventually, you must say good-bye at the end of an evening. Don't just slip out. It's a question of practice.

The art of moving your orbit more centrally, visualizing how you want to be seen, speaking early and remembering the structure of conversations, and using your people color zone reading skills are the basics of accessing your gravitas.

All of the constructs are at play in a social engagement especially if you find your courage and confidence seem low. The temperaments begin with being comfortable in your own skin and identity, and letting the somatic Self 2 do the leading. Your courage to be authentic, maintain dignity, and poise in the credibility construct will get you noticed and feed your confidence. And finally, when you are in a conversation try moving the mood of the others and the climate of the group to have some hand on control, and you will begin to build the gravitas you crave.

Chapter Twelve

Situations: Strategies and Tactics
Part Two – Presentations

The art of presenting is the subject of hundreds or perhaps thousands of books, online guides, businesses, and courses. It is not surprising given that it is one of the most common situations that people fear. As I have shared many times throughout the book I am more introverted than extroverted, but I have very rarely been paralyzed by the fear of speaking in public and I am able to use my 'out of preference' facet of expressiveness to hopefully try to engage others. However, that doesn't mean that before every speaking or teaching engagement I don't experience anxiety or worse.

Before we move specifically on to the art or arts of speaking in public I want to begin with the subject of anxiety and panic attacks. My story actually begins with the latter, panic. If you have never had a panic attack this part may feel a little alien but I can assure you that for anyone who has experienced one it is very real and genuinely terrifying. I found myself reading Prince Harry's book, *Spare*, the other day, and was surprised to read about him giving speeches during a panic attack. Perhaps we don't expect others, especially in the public eye with a lifetime of training, to experience something that we might and in some ways that should be reassuring. In the fictional series from Apple, *Ted Lasso*, played wonderfully by the actor Jason Sudeikis, Ted experiences a severe panic attack in the first season, and he does what anyone who experiences panic feels the need to do, escape from others. He sits alone wringing his hands tightly and his emotions are pouring out. It's extremely moving and a very accurate interpretation of how a panic attack feels.

Anxiety and Panic Attacks

My experience with panic really began in childhood, but it wasn't diagnosed or understood by a specialist and didn't have an impact on my adult life until I was 29 years old. I was on a summer vacation having just attended the 1996 Atlanta Olympic Games accompanying a group of students studying Event Management from George Washington University. After the Games I went to San Francisco to stay with a friend before hoping to travel to British Columbia and Alberta in Canada where I had worked a few years earlier, at the Banff Springs Hotel. I recall telephoning an airline to organize my flight to Vancouver and there was a bit of a problem with the booking. Not an unusual situation for any of us but whilst I was talking I found myself struggling to breathe. It got worse and worse and eventually I couldn't speak, and my head became so busy with thoughts that I couldn't hear how the call was going and I had to hang up. It left me exhausted and confused. I hadn't started the call like that but was unable to finish it, and I felt kind of inexplicably emotional at the end.

Eventually, I did get to Canada and started to make my journey from Vancouver to Calgary. En route I stayed in a hostel when the same physiological symptoms hit me from nowhere. My head went very light and I could feel my brain clouding, my breathing racing, my chest almost exploding whilst I was out for dinner with some friends. I carried on speaking to them but couldn't remember what I was saying and couldn't eat any more and felt trapped. They noticed nothing but I knew I had to get out and so I did. I went to my room in emotional distress making an excuse that I didn't feel well. The next day I was out shopping, and it happened again whilst I was with a friend, and I literally panicked as I felt I was going to have a heart attack. I went to the ER at the local hospital and they checked everything before their conclusion, "You've had a panic attack." And, "It's nothing to worry about." Actually it was, but not immediately. Their diagnosis helped reassure me for just one month.

About a week before I was due to return to work lecturing at college again and just one month after the Canada trip, I started to feel the symptoms as a passenger in a car. And then again in a cinema, and again in restaurants. By now I was super alert to the warning signs and simply saying panic attack made it worse. I noticed that every time one struck me I had to escape. And, after each one I cried, privately. I thought, I am finished. This will never end — I can't teach again.

I went to see a specialist who explained the mechanics of what happens and understandably started working on breathing techniques. However, they were not working. Once the panic grip begins it is simply impossible to logically focus on a breathing process — it's too late. I delayed my start of teaching explaining to the head of department a few misleading illness problems, but luckily, she was kind. However, I had to do something. This was before the Internet was there to help — or not! So, I purchased every book possible to become a self-expert. The problem, however, about panic is that once you start thinking about, reading about it, or even writing about it, like now, it can feel like it's trying to engineer itself back into your life. I have also found that when I teach about the subject in groups, the same things happen to some others. The paradox emerges that trying to help people with panic can actually bring panic on initially, and it is a painful process to overcome.

However, let me begin this paragraph by saying that I have. And I want to explain how because if you can get through panic, working with anxiety is easy. Initially I went through these huge cognitive behavioral therapy workbooks but none of them helped. And then I purchased a tiny little self-help book on living with panic. The sort of book I could take anywhere. It's called *Your Survival Guide to Panic Attacks* by Bev Aisbett and it's brilliant. Anyway, up until that point I just wanted to get rid of my panic, but this little book referred to my panic as 'IT' and in my head 'my little dragon.' It was mostly full of images rather than words, throughout, and the dragon was a small purple fire-breathing dragon with teeth and a bit of a cheeky smile that followed me everywhere on my shoulder. It didn't go away but I could quieten it down, I could talk to it. IT had a face. And if IT did IT couldn't take over me for more than 15 minutes. After that IT would stop taking over my mind. At the time just accepting that IT was always there made me feel better, but it also taught me some other things that IT didn't like. IT didn't like to be distracted by me moving around — using my larger muscle groups. IT had told me it preferred me when I was trapped. That's why restaurants, cinemas, aircraft were all wonderful for IT because it was not so easy for me to escape. A martial arts expert friend of mine taught me a trick as well. Panic hates physical pain and he showed me how to hurt myself quietly so as to quieten down panic. He told me dig my thumbnail on to my little finger cuticle and press hard. It hurts. When you did it, if you sensed panic rising it distracts you. The breathing and focus pay attention to the finger pain. I know someone that used to push a drawing pin into their thigh — I wouldn't recommend it as it can bleed, but it worked for them. It's a somatic Self 2 technique and it works. Panic is a Self 1 thinking process that constantly scans the horizon for more reasons to panic and becomes good at it. So, if you suffer from panic or high anxiety here are some things you must start to do:

1. Exercise. Get fitter. With lower blood pressure, increased blood flow, and the dopamine that accompanies exercise you will not only feel more alive but also less likely to have breathing problems, and muscles remember quickly what activity and benefit of movement feels like. Nobody likes to be told this of course!

2. Walk regularly at work, especially before any situation which you have a fear of. The big muscle groups, your legs, and glutes must move, and as they do they make you feel more relaxed. You are moving from paralysis to action.
3. Concentrate on relaxing through the hips and tail bone. Remember your tension will build from here.
4. Practice and use diaphragmatic breathing and the 4-5-7 breathing technique: Inhale, hold, exhale.
5. Relax behind the eyes.
6. Place the tip of your tongue on the roof of your mouth gently.
7. If you start to have an attack and you can move, such as presenting on a stage, move; if you can't because you are seated and somewhere static — hurt yourself, just enough so long as you don't cry out!
8. Tell your IT dragon to be quiet.
9. Finally, don't be ashamed of asking for medical help. A lot of people with a panic condition who have professions which require them to perform and have no escape use a beta-blocker. They don't fix panic, they are not addictive, and do not affect brain functioning. For example, I know of a few orchestral musicians who have to perform in just such environments and have severe panic worry. They will take a single beta blocker around half an hour before a performance and it helps. It simply stops the heart rate from increasing too high which in turn can help quieten the mind as it hunts for cues to get your dragon excited. Clearly it is not suitable for sports athletes. Just remember to talk to a medical professional first please.

At a different level anxiety is much more common and is something that everyone has from time to time, but it is manageable by working on points 1 through 6 just as is recommended for panic.

The other recommendation I cited earlier is Susan Jeffers' book, *Feel the Fear and Do It Anyway*. The reason is that anxiety often comes from a fear, and often fear is driven by thought patterns and language patters such 'what if this happens.' It is the use of negative thinking and language that leads to worry and anxiety. She refers to the language shift from 'Pain to Power.' For example:

From: Pain Language = Helplessness = Depression = Paralysis
Replaced with: Power Language = Choice = Excitement = Action
In vocabulary for example replace:

From: I can't	To: I won't
From: I should	To: I could/will
From: It's not my fault	To: I am completely responsible
From: It's a problem	To: It's an opportunity
From: Life's a struggle	To: Life's an adventure
From: I hope	To: I know
From: If only	To: Next time
From: What will I do	To: I know I can handle it

In summary, the presentation situation is a classic theater where we can often experience terrifying panic or highly damaging anxiety. When these take over it becomes impossible to focus on having gravitas through any of the constructs of temperaments. The presentation is where Self 1 critical thinking, judgement thinking, negative self-talk, and somatic tension thrive. But rather than talk your way through all of it focus on somatic conditioning, imagery, movement, and you will be fine.

Returning to the presentation situation.

Situation:
- Is this a presentation that requires gravitas?
- What is your gravitas goal with this presentation?

Environment:
- What color is the environment in which the presentation will take place?
- What zone color are the people you need to influence?
- Which zone are you in?
- What way do you need to move the color zone to be effective?

Tactics:
There are some very useful tactics before and during a presentation which allow all of your constructs to shine.

The first one is not always something you will have access to, but I'll share it with you. I want you to learn a technique that will make you feel heavy in your shoes, like Neil Armstrong's moon walking boots. They will stop you floating away. I discovered it through the writing of Dinh, Lord, and Hoffman (2014) who provided an example of how holding a heavy object can convey a feeling of weight, and can make the perception of others and situations feel more important. Try to find a heavy weight to store where you work — something like an old dumbbell. You want a weight of around 10 kg or 20+ lb. Try this:

- Pick it up and try walking around with it for a minute. Put it down and walk. Pick it up again and do the same.
- What do you notice?
- You should feel as though your feet are heavier and the weight is still there.

As I said this may not be easy if you are travelling or haven't any private space, but it works. Another approach is to purchase some ankle strap weights to practice with but remember to take them off before you actually present as it can create a very odd visual effect to those who are listening! You might also try lifting your desk as an alternative, or when you are at home, practice with any heavy weight and then visualize the weight prior to speaking as that will help too.

The last of the somatic tactics draws on the strongest of your senses, the sense of smell. As you may remember reading earlier, smell is powerful because it provides the shortest route to the feeling and decision-making functions of the brain. I first developed the technique in Australia delivering a program on storytelling techniques. I purchased a box of 30 specimen jars — usually used in hospitals — but I placed in each one a different product with a distinct smell. I used peanut butter, freshly cut grass, Marmite or Vegemite (very British-Aussie, I know), coffee, tea, sandalwood oil, cinnamon, marzipan, disinfectant, soap, curry powder, sun tan lotion, tiger balm, and I think some type of tree scent. My group could go to a table and smell all of them but when they found a smell that invoked a memory they would tell a story. It turned out to be an incredibly powerful tool, and I had made it up as an activity with no idea if it would work. However, much later as I developed the technique further I found that some people would describe how certain smells made them feel different, sometimes calmer or happier, and sometimes more anxious. For example, one person after smelling disinfectant was immediately reminded of being in the hospital with their mother dying. Something I had to be very careful about in the future so as not to expose too much psychological danger.

Eventually though, I focused only on developing smells that made people feel good, that took them somewhere pleasant, and helped them to relax. As my coaching practice evolved my clients learnt to identify five smells that took them to a good place, and they would carry these jars around with them and use them to relax before stressful situations or as part of a daily meditative practice.

Therefore, I recommend that you do the same when preparing to present or invoke courage in a stressful situation. Find five smells and keep them in your jars somewhere safe; take some time to breathe in through the nose, hold, and then slowly out through the mouth for one minute before you engage others. You will need to refresh the jars if their odor disappears of course.

Messages and Storytelling

All of the somatic activities similarly apply to presenting but to deliver your message in a structured way I am going to point you in the direction of something called 'sticky messages.' It comes from some research and practice that Chip and Dan Heath wrote in a book called *Made to Stick*. They researched thousands of talks, sayings, phrases, stories that people seemed to remember, and identified six reasons why some are so effective and memorable.

Firstly, the six important ingredients are:

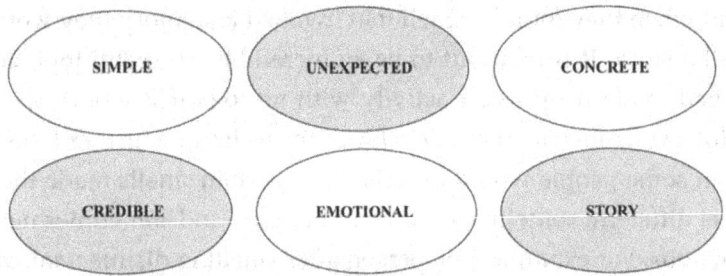

Figure 12.1: The Six Ingredients for 'Sticky Messages' (Heath and Heath, 2007)

Firstly, your message needs to be simple:

- Find the core of the idea.
- Some ideas you weed out may be important. But you must find the one that is most important and build your story around that.
- Identify critical wins rather than just beneficial.
- Avoid burying the lead. Don't start with something interesting but irrelevant. Work to make the core message itself more interesting.

Secondly, it needs to be somewhat unexpected in a way that gets attention:

- Get attention by breaking a pattern.
- Surprise gets attention; interest holds it.
- Once you have the core, figure out what is counterintuitive about the message (unexpected implications, for example).
- Break your audience's guessing machine along that counterintuitive dimension.

It also needs to be unexpected so that it holds attention:

- Create a mystery or some other mental journey on which your audience wants to go.
- Curiosity happens when we feel a gap in our knowledge. Create that gap and draw the audience into the process of closing it.
- Highlight specific knowledge they are missing, alert them to their need for it, and then provide it in measured, distributed bits.

Thirdly, it needs to be what they refer to as 'concrete,' which means:

- Try to paint a visual image.
- Use all the senses to make your point.

Fourthly, it needs to be put together in such a way that it is credible, it feels real:

- Credible ideas speak for themselves.
- Use credible sources or people.
- Consider, what level of credibility do you have for what you need to say and do?

The fifth one is finding an emotional connection:

- For people to act, they have to care.
- Analytical thinking by itself may actually reduce the propensity to act.
- Appeal to people's self-interest and their identities.
- Associate your ideas with other ideas already cared about.
- Create empathy for specific individuals.

And the last one is a story with a structure:

- We learn best from experience.
- A story simulates experience.
- Stories create empathy.
- It has to have a point!

The structures I have worked with are a hybrid version of Kurt Vonnegut's curve and from Robert McKee's brilliant book on screenplay writing called *Story*. In essence story structures seem to reflect a series of similarly shaped curves that look a little like a wave or the curves on an oscilloscope. Vonnegut called these "The Shapes of Stories." In fact his theory was presented in his anthropology master's thesis, which was rejected because it was too simplistic. I find that somewhat astonishing as I emphasized much earlier that so many of the sciences' primary aim is to find elegant, simple overarching means of explaining something to everyone. Anyway, one way I have found to use the curve is to focus on the three-part structure of a conventional story. It is one which you will have seen over and over again in movies. Perhaps not some of the more Indie styles and certainly not a Bollywood movie as one of my students reminded me once!

In effect the three parts are captured in the image of a wave in the sea building as it gains momentum towards the shore. As the wave builds and momentum moves forwards the wave gathers in height until it reaches its maximum height before crashing down and rolling in towards the shore. Each of the parts is equal in length. The beginning, the middle, and the end. Ask yourself, how many times have you seen a presentation where there is a quick buildup, then most of the time spent in the middle, and an almost abrupt end. I've seen thousands, and used this technique to improve the quality of structure and ultimately help to ensure the communication construct has real gravitas. Whether you speak for 3 minutes, 15, or 30, the approach is the same and reflects the flow of a movie.

A typical movie lasts around 90 minutes and is split into 3 x 30 minutes with significant plot points. In the first 30 minutes we meet the main characters and get to know their situation and an introduction to the plot. At 30 minutes an incident occurs where a major struggle of some sort take place where we don't know what will happen next. In the second phase we get into what is called 'the struggle between expectation and cruel reality.' The 'what' will happen in the next phase. At the 60 minute point a key incident happens again where we find out the answer to that, and see how it unfolds in the final 30 minutes as it reaches its conclusion.

When presenting in business use the same three parts:

1. Build a picture of what you will cover, why it should matter, and the hurdles and challenges ahead.
2. Now build that as a struggle between all that will have to be done but the reality of how it might play out. The so-called struggle between expectation and cruel reality.
3. Find the wow moment of what was achieved or the hope and excitement of what comes next whilst you tailor down to the conclusions and actions ahead.

The wave or curve also reflects your energy, and as you explain the situation, get excitement into the room and then bring people alongside you. In effect it often looks like building a red zone of energy initially to make some movement into a static environment before building in a slower blue zone, and then raising the tempo again to a green or red zone before heading finally back to green to reengage your audience. If your more preferred introverted blue state makes it difficult to engage a red energy, project your calmer green to individuals in the audience using your uniqueness to engage individuals and once a few of them connect with you the energy will build to effect the climate or mood you desire, giving you control. Lastly, practice. Record yourself as I have recommended before presenting or speaking on any topic, and have the courage to look at the recording until you feel good about yourself.

End

Wrapping Up: The Final Piece of the Gravitas Jigsaw
Developing gravitas with the help of your inner coach is a process that takes time. I have proposed the idea that you work with your inner visual and somatic coach primarily, so that when you practice your gravitas it will have more of a sense of feeling and copying your role models rather than one where you have to remember 20 steps. Most professional coaching activities in business are conducted in a seated one to one setting with a focus on cognition, and really this is at odds with how effective coaching works.

I have written the book with the angle of helping the more introverted build their gravitas as this is where my experiences lie, but they are still effective for the more extroverted and also can apply out of the workplace. The introverted tend to have more of the challenges of building their courage and confidence, especially with others, but I hope I have also demonstrated they have advantages in building trust and credibility. Learning to control oneself is the starting point to controlling the mood of others and the climate you wish to build. Ultimately the way we communicate often becomes the means of how others will interpret our gravitas and the way in which you become skilled takes practice and focus.

Therefore, I ask you to return to the goals you set in the section on "Knowing Your Gravitas." Since you wrote those down we added a series of tools around color awareness of situations and people, and examples of situations, strategies, and tactics to employ. Find those original goals you set and rewrite them to include the color modeling and tactics I have shared in the final chapter.

And, so I draw the book to a close and ask that you go and play. Work on your goals and experiment with your tactics and keep a note of your successes and failures.

Good luck, and remember:

One day, in retrospect, the years of struggle will strike you as the most beautiful.
— Sigmund Freud (1960)

References

Adler, A. (1924). *The Practice and Theory of Individual Psychology* (trans. Radin, P.). New York: Harcourt, Brace and Company.

Agle, B.R. et al. (2006). Does CEO charisma Matter? An Empirical Analysis of the Relationships Among Organizational Performance, Environmental Uncertainty and Top Management Team Perception of CEO Charisma. *Academy of Management Journal*, 49, pp. 161–174.

Aguilera-Barchet, B. (2015). *A History of Western Public Law*. Cham: Springer International Publishing.

Aisbett, B. (1998). *Your Survival Guide to Panic Attacks*. London: HarperCollins Publishers.

Apuzzo, M.L. (2006). Gravitas, Severitas, Veritas, Virtus. *Neurosurgery*, 59(2), pp. 219–221.

Arendt, H. (1993). *Between Past and Future: Eight Exercises in Political Thought*. London: Penguin.

Avolio, B.J. (2005). *Leadership Development in Balance: Made/Born*. Mahwah, NJ: Lawrence Erlbaum.

Avolio, B.J. and Gardner, W.L. (2005). Authentic leadership development: Getting to the root of positive forms of leadership. *Leadership Quarterly*, 16(3), pp. 315–338.

Avolio, B.J., Gardner, W.L., Walumbwa, F.O., Wernsing, T.S., and Peterson, S.J. (2008). Authentic Leadership: Development and Validation of a Theory-Based Measure†. *Journal of Management*, 34(1), pp. 89–126.

Avolio, B.J., Gardner, W.L., Walumbwa, F.O., Luthans, F., and May, D.R. (2004). Unlocking the Mask: A Look at the Process by Which Authentic Leaders Impact Follower Attitudes and Behaviors. *Leadership Quarterly*, 15: 801–823.

Avolio, B.J. and Luthans, F. (2006). *The High Impact Leader: Moments Matter in Accelerating Authentic Leadership Development*. New York: McGraw-Hill.

Baron, L. and Parent, E. (2014). Developing Authentic Leadership Within a Training Context: Three Phenomena Supporting the Individual Development Process. *Journal of Leadership and Organizational Studies*, 1–17. Sage Publications.

Bass, M. and Bass, R. (2008). *The Bass Handbook of Leadership: Theory, Research, and Managerial Applications*, Fourth Edition. New York: Free Press.

Broussine, M. and Fox, P. (2002). Rethinking Leadership in Local Government: The Place of 'Feminine' Styles in the Modernised Council. *Local Government Studies*, 28(4).

Corkindale, G. (2007). In Search of Gravitas. *Harvard Business Review*. Available at: https://hbr.org/2007/05/in-search-of-gravitas/ (Accessed: 3 November 2011).

Cox, B. (Prof.) and Cohen, A. (2015). *Human Universe*. Glasgow: Williams Collins.

Dagley, G.R. and Gaskin, C.J. (2014). Understanding executive presence: Perspectives of business professionals. *Consulting Psychology Journal: Practice and Research*, 66(3), p. 197.

Damasio, A. (1994). Descartes' *Error: Emotion, Reason and the Human Brain*. New York: Putnam.

De Rivera, J. (ed.). (1981). *Conceptual Encounter: A method for the exploration of human experience*. Lanham, MD: University Press of America.

Dinh, J.E., Lord, R.G., and Hoffman, E. (2014). Leadership Perception and Information Processing: Influences of Symbolic, Connectionist, Emotional, and Embodied Architectures. In *The Oxford Handbook of Leadership and Organizations*. Oxford University Press, p. 305.

Duignan, P. (2002). August. The Catholic Educational Leader: Defining authentic leadership: veritas, caristas, and gravitas.

In *International Conference: Vision and Reality*. Sydney: Australian Catholic University, pp. 4–7.

Eagly, A.H. (2005). Achieving Relational Authenticity in Leadership: Does Gender Matter? *Leadership Quarterly*, 16(3), pp. 459–474.

Erickson, R.J. (1995). The Importance of Authenticity for Self and Society. *Symbolic Interaction*, 18(2), pp. 121–144.

Fairhurst, G.T. (2005). Reframing the Art of Framing: Problems and Prospects for Leadership. *Leadership*, 1(2), pp. 165–185.

Fanelli, A. and Misangyi, V.F. (2006). Bringing out Charisma: CEO Charisma and External Stakeholders. *Academy of Management Review*, 31(4), pp. 1049–1061.

For the Love of Spock. (2016). Film, Adam Nimoy, USA, 455 Films.

Gallwey, W.T. (1975). *The Inner Game of Tennis*. London: Nicholas Brealey Publishing.

Gardiner, Rita A. (2011). Critique of the discourse of authentic leadership. *International Journal of Business and Social Science*, 2.15 (2011): 99.

Goffee, R. and Jones, G. (2006). *Why Should Anyone Be Led by You? What It Takes to Be an Authentic Leader*. London: Harvard Business Press.

Grant, E. (1996). *The Foundation of Modern Science in the Middle Ages: Their Religious, Institutional and Intellectual Contexts*. Cambridge: Cambridge University Press.

Guignon, C.B. (2004). *On Being Authentic*. Psychology Press.

Harter, S. (2002). Authenticity. In Snyder, C.R. and Lopez, S.J. (eds.), *Handbook of Positive Psychology*, 382–394. London: Oxford University Press.

Heath, C. and Heath, D. (2007). *Made to Stick: Why Some Ideas Survive and Others Die*. New York: Random House.

Hemingway, E. (2018). JFK and Hemingway: Beyond "Grace under Pressure." Available at: https://jfk.blogs.archives.gov/2018/07/20/jfk-hemingway (Accessed: 31 August 2022).

Jeffers, S. (1987). *Feel the Fear and Do It Anyway*. New York: Harcourt Brace Jovanovich.

Jeffers, S. (2007). *Feel the Fear and Do It Anyway: How to Turn Your Fear and Indecision into Confidence and Action*. London: Vermilion.

Jung, C. (1923). *Psychological Types*. New York: Harcourt, Brace and Company.

Kamtekar, R. (2010). Marcus Aurelius. In *The Stanford Encyclopedia of Philosophy*. Edited by Edward N. Zalta. Stanford, CA: Stanford University.

Kernis, M.H. (2003). Toward a Conceptualization of Optimal Self-Esteem. *Psychological Inquiry*, 14(1), pp. 1–26.

Kets de Vries, M.F.R. (2015). Finding Gravitas | INSEAD Knowledge. 2016. Available at: http://knowledge.insead.edu/blog/insead-blog/finding-gravitas-4248 (Accessed: 10 January 2016).

Klaas, B. (2022). Why we always get the wrong political leaders – and how to get the right ones. *The Sunday Times*, 15 January.

Klein, K.J. and House, R.J. (1995). On Fire: Charismatic leaders and levels of analysis. *Leadership Quarterly*, 6: 183–198.

Kolb, D. (1984). *Experiential Learning*. Englewood Cliffs, NJ: Prentice-Hall.

Ladkin, D. and Taylor, S.S. (2010). Enacting the 'true self': Towards a theory of embodied authentic leadership. *Leadership Quarterly*, 21(1), pp. 64–74.

Landau, M.J., Meier, B.P., and Keefer, L.A. (2010). A metaphor-enriched social cognition. *Psychological Bulletin*, 136, 1045–1067. doi:10.1037/a0020970.

Laney, M.O. (2002). *The Introvert Advantage: How to Thrive in an Extrovert World*. New York: Workman Publishing.

Lindholm, C. (2008). *Culture and Authenticity*. Malden, MA: Wiley-Blackwell.

Macaux, W. (2013). Gravitas: A latent variable in executive presence. Available at: http://generativityllc/blog/Gravitas (Accessed: 8 April 2015).

Maister, D., Green, C., and Galford, R. (2001). *The Trusted Advisor*. New York: The Free Press.

Maslow, A. (1943). A Theory of Human Motivation. *Motivation and Personality*.

Matthews, T. (2013). More than a brain on legs: An exploration of working with the body in coaching. *International Journal of Evidence Based Coaching and Mentoring*, Special Issue 7, pp. 26–38.

McKay, B. and McKay, K. (2017). Lessons from Walter Cronkite in the Lost Art of Gravitas. Available at: https://www.artofmanliness.com/character/manly-lessons/lessons-walter-cronkite-lost-art-gravitas/ (Accessed: 2 December 2021).

McKee, R. (1997). *Story: Substance, Structure, Style, and the Principles of Screenwriting*. New York: Regan Books.

Meier, B.P., Schnall, S., Schwarz, N., and Bargh, J.A. (2012). Embodiment in social psychology. *Topics in Cognitive Science*, 4(4), pp. 705–716.

Monarth, H. (2010). *Executive Presence: The Art of Commanding Respect Like a CEO*. New York: McGraw-Hill.

Morrow, L. (1988). Essay: The Gravitas Factor. *Time* magazine. Available at: http://content.time.com/time/magazine/article/0,9171,966995,00.htm (Accessed: 4 October 2011).

Naidoo, L.J. and Lord, R.G. (2008). Speech imagery and perceptions of charisma: The mediating role of positive affect. *Leadership Quarterly*, 19(3), pp. 283–296.

Nørretranders, T. (1998). *The User Illusion: Cutting Consciousness Down to Size*, trans. Jonathan Sydenham. New York: Viking Penguin.

Pedersen, O. (1993). *Early Physics and Astronomy*. Cambridge: Cambridge University Press, p. 130.

Ratener, M. (2014). Quoted by Goodell, C., 2014, Somatic Markers in Clinical Practice. In *Psychology Applications & Developments*, edited by Clara Pracana, Advances in Psychology and Psychological Trends Series. InScience Press, p. 85.

Rodenburg, P. (2007). *Presence: How to Use Positive Energy for Success in Every Situation*. London: Penguin.

Rogers, C.R. (1951). *Client-Centered Therapy: Its Current Practice, Implications and Theory*. Boston: Houghton Mifflin.

Seligman, M.E. and Csikszentmihalyi, M. (2000). Positive psychology: An introduction. *American Psychological Association*, Vol. 55, No. 1, p. 5.

Sieler, A. (2010). Ontological Coaching. In Cox, E., Bachkirova, T., and Clutterbuck, D.A., *The Complete Handbook of Coaching*. London: Sage.

Taleb, N. (2010). *The Black Swan: The Impact of the Highly Improbable*. New York: Random House.

Trilling, L. (1972). *Sincerity and Authenticity*. London: Oxford University Press.

Ware, C. (2014). The *Severitas* of Constantine: Imperial Virtues in *Panegyrici Latini* 7(6) and 6(7). *Journal of Late Antiquity*, 7(1), pp. 86–109.

Western, S. (2012). *Coaching and Mentoring: A Critical Text*. London: Sage.

Whitmore, J. (1992). *Coaching for Performance: GROWing human potential and purpose: the principles and practice of coaching and leadership*. London: Nicholas Brealey.

Wilson, M. (2002). Six views of embodied cognition. *Psychonomic Bulletin & Review*, 9(4), pp. 625–636.

Yukl, G.A. (1981, 2001, and 2002). *Leadership in Organizations*. Englewood Cliffs, NJ: Prentice-Hall.

About the Author

Ian accidentally discovered an interest in gravitas having previously taught executive presence, leadership, conducting psychometric assessments, and helping people manage anxiety and panic syndrome. He always felt there was something missing from coaching presence, something unseen that was a combination of both magnetism and depth of character. He subsequently became the first person to research and receive a doctorate in coaching for gravitas in a leadership context anywhere in the world. He found that there was a need for gravitas in his own work but it was often inaccessible, and he wanted to understand why gravitas is so hard to find and why it evaporated quickly when some needed it the most. He uncovered hundreds of similar stories from others and was dedicated to help people overcome their personal barriers to performance that hindered any effective gravitas they hoped to acquire. He worked with leaders to co-develop approaches that could be self-managed through a form of inner coaching. Many of them were more introverted, just as Ian was, and it occurred to him that he should orientate his writing towards some of their unique challenges but also their advantages in a very extroverted world.

Ian's career began in the 1980s when he joined the UK Royal Air Force, working in tactics and trials. This was followed by various degrees ranging from sport and leisure, adult education, and development through to coaching psychology, supporting his next role as a senior lecturer in higher education. He subsequently moved into the private sector, initially as a training manager for a small car company and then as a senior executive leader with Rolls-Royce and then Bentley Motors, where he was responsible for their global academy, and part of the team that launched their Continental GT car. Afterwards he emigrated to Australia and became a Director with PwC (Price Waterhouse Coopers) in their advisory and consulting arm. He became self-employed in 2006, initially working with the Australian Graduate School of Management and then returned to London where he was contracted as an Ambassador Educator with Duke Corporate Education whilst also continuing advisory work for specialist consulting firms. His clients have ranged from junior talent, leaders of multinational corporations, women leaders in the Middle East, newspaper editors, heads of television and digital media, aircraft engineers through to mining geologists working in remote areas of the world.

He temporarily moved to the USA in 2019 and then to Mexico in 2020 during the Covid-19 pandemic where he focused on writing despite being constantly slowed down with an eye disease which meant he often could only really see clearly through one eye. He moved permanently to the USA in 2023 with his American wife, Erin, three stepchildren, and his English Springer Spaniel, and continues to focus on writing, coaching, and mentoring. He holds both British and Australian nationalities.

BUSINESS
BOOKS

Business Books

Business Books publishes practical guides
and insightful non-fiction for beginners and professionals.
Covering aspects from management skills, leadership and
organizational change to positive work environments, career
coaching and self-care for managers, our books are a valuable
addition to those working in the world of business.

Recent Bestsellers from Business Books Are:

From 50 to 500
Jonathan Dapra, Richard Dapra and Jonas Akerman
An engaging and innovative small business leadership framework guaranteed to strengthen a leader's effectiveness to drive company growth and results.
Paperback: 978-1-78904-743-1 ebook: 978-1-78904-744-8

Be Visionary
Marty Strong
Be Visionary: Strategic Leadership in the Age of Optimization demonstrates to existing and aspiring leaders the positive impact of applying visionary creativity and decisiveness to achieve spectacular long-range results while balancing the day-to-day.
Paperback: 978-1-78535-432-8 ebook: 978-1-78535-433-5

Finding Sustainability
Trent A. Romer
Journey to eight states, three national parks and three countries to experience the life-changing education that led Trent A. Romer to find sustainability for his plastic-bag manufacturing business and himself.
Paperback: 978-1-78904-601-4 ebook: 978-1-78904-602-1

Inner Brilliance, Outer Shine
Estelle Read
Optimise your success, performance, productivity and well-being to lead your best business life.
Paperback: 978-1-78904-803-2 ebook: 978-1-78904-804-9

Tomorrow's Jobs Today
Rafael Moscatel and Abby Jane Moscatel
Discover leadership secrets and technology strategies being pioneered by today's most innovative business executives and renowned brands across the globe.
Paperback: 978-1-78904-561-1 ebook: 978-1-78904-562-8

Secrets to Successful Property Investment
Deb Durbin
Your complete guide to building a property portfolio.
Paperback: 978-1-78904-818-6 ebook: 978-1-78904-819-3

The Effective Presenter
Ryan Warriner
The playbook to professional presentation success!
Paperback: 978-1-78904-795-0 ebook: 978-1-78904-796-7

The Beginner's Guide to Managing
Mikil Taylor
A how-to guide for first-time managers adjusting to their new leadership roles.
Paperback: 978-1-78904-583-3 ebook: 978-1-78904-584-0

Forward
Elizabeth Moran
A practical playbook for leaders to guide their teams through their organization's next big change.
Paperback: 978-1-78279-289-5 ebook: 978-1-78279-291-8

Readers of ebooks can buy or view any of these bestsellers by clicking on the live link in the title. Most titles are published in paperback and as an ebook. Paperbacks are available in traditional bookshops. Both print and ebook formats are available online.

Find more titles and sign up to our readers' newsletter at
www.collectiveinkbooks.com/business-books